D1569334

Writing
For
Business

*Helpful, Easy-to-Apply Advice
for Everyone Who Writes on the Job*

Stephen Wilbers, Ph.D.

The Good Writing Press,
Minneapolis

Printed in the United States of America

First published in 1993

Second edition 2007

Library of Congress Cataloging in Publication Data:
93-070112

ISBN: 0-9635995-0-X

The Good Writing Press
4828 Tenth Avenue South
Minneapolis, MN 55417-1163

My thanks to Debbie, Eddy, and Kate for their love, to my parents, brothers, sisters, and friends for their care, to my men's group for their interest, to my running pals for their stamina, to my writing friends for their courage, to my students for their spirit, to my editors for their forbearance, and to my readers for their commitment to precise use of language.

Note to the second edition

After 35 years of teaching and nearly 16 years of meeting a weekly deadline, I feel like an old hand at offering advice to writers. But when I was getting started back in 1991 every new column seemed like an insurmountable challenge. Would I run out of ideas? Could I make the next column as good as, or better than, the previous one? Column by column, my anxiety and relief knew no boundaries. (Tomorrow I'll write my 732nd column.)

When my readers told me they found my advice not only helpful but also entertaining, I was encouraged, and in my enthusiasm I self-published my first 50 columns. My readers responded to my collection with further encouragement, and, to my astonishment, it won a 1994 Minnesota Book Award. With this second edition I am pleased to bring these columns back into print. I hope you enjoy reading them.

Stephen Wilbers,
May 6, 2007

Table of Contents

Writing with Emphasis

Writing as Process

Writing in Delicate Situations

Works Cited / Recommended Reading

Introduction

Competence often measured by ability to reach others

Most of you who write on the job don't write with the intent of establishing your reputations as great writers. You have a more pragmatic purpose in mind. You write to get the job done.

Even so, you no doubt appreciate the importance of good writing – writing that is clear, concise, and correct. And you probably know (perhaps fear?) that your competence is judged, at least in part, by the quality of your writing.

As management expert Peter Drucker reminds us, "As soon as you move one step up from the bottom, your effectiveness depends on your ability to reach others through the spoken or written word."

Author William Zinsser says it more bluntly: "Bad writing makes bright people look dumb."

The purpose of these columns is to help make bright people look bright.

Here's my premise: Whether your writing skills are relatively strong or weak, you can take steps to improve your writing. I believe you can always get better (or worse – but let's take the positive view here).

What can you do to become a better writer? Simple. Read good writers and work with good teachers. OK. Nothing new there. Let's assume that you've spent the better part of your formative years doing just that. Now you're an adult and you want a little review and maybe a few pointers on how to continue to improve your writing.

What's your next step? Take a refresher course, naturally. As a bright and capable person, it's the least that you can do.

Here's what I'm offering: In each column I'll give you some practical but light-hearted advice on how to apply the basic principles of good writing to the writing you do on the job. I'll begin with some techniques for writing clearly, concisely, and correctly, and we'll move on from there. Whether you love to write or hate to write, I think you'll find my tips helpful. Who knows? We may even have some fun. So, let's get started.

Writing Clearly

To keep your readers' attention, get to the point

Let's face it. Business writing is not generally read by an enraptured, adoring audience. It's read by busy people who for the most part would rather be doing something else.

After all, that's why they call it "business" writing, isn't it?

I know. That's hard to accept. The truth hurts. But – we may as well go ahead and get it over with – the cold, painful reality is this: If your readers weren't getting paid to read your writing, they probably wouldn't do it.

Given this unfortunate state of affairs, you can't afford to fool around. To keep your readers' attention, you need to present your ideas and information in a style that is clear, concise, and to the point. You don't have the luxury of wasting your readers' time.

Perhaps the most costly mistake you can make in business writing is failing to make yourself clear. So, what can you do to ensure that your readers get your message?

Well, a number of things. You can work with sentence structure, paragraph structure, word choice, and organization, among others. But on the most basic level, you can simply make certain that you tell your readers why you are writing, and do it right away – if not in the first sentence, then in the first paragraph.

In other words, begin your document with your most important information. Lead off with a statement of purpose. Don't bury your main points in the middle of the third or fourth paragraph.

And while we're on the topic of paragraphs, you would be well advised to keep your first one short. A long, involved opening paragraph is daunting to readers. The message you risk sending with a lead-off paragraph of five or six sentences, as opposed to a paragraph of two or three, is: "Be prepared to slow down, hold off on whatever else you need to do, concentrate on this, and work hard."

For certain types of writing, this may be just the message you want to send. But in today's fast-paced business world, it's almost always better to begin with a short, quick opening, a fast start that invites your readers into the document with the promise, "Don't worry. It's an easy ride. I'll move you through this material quickly and expeditiously. Let's get going."

One way to ensure that you are stating your purpose clearly and getting to the point quickly is to use a formula a colleague of mine once told me about. It's a formula for writing a 3-step memo.

Here's how it works. The next time you sit down to write a memo, try organizing your thoughts into three paragraphs, beginning with these phrases:

"I am writing because. . ."
"The main points are. . ."
"I propose that you. . ."

It's almost impossible to complete these phrases without being clear and explicit about your reason for writing.

If you find that this approach works for you, that it helps get you off to a quick start, you may want to create a macro on your computer and have these cues appear on command so that never again will you have to face the terror of a blank screen.

But remember: The 3-step formula is only a jump start. You still need to drive the car.

After you have your memo under way, you may want to go back and change your lead sentences to make them more interesting and less abrupt. You may also decide to provide additional background information in an attachment. But by beginning with this formula, you greatly increase your chances of writing clearly.

How do *you* define effective business writing?

Ask any group of business writers to write down two words or phrases that describe effective business writing, and the vast majority of them will come up with the same words.

Don't believe me? Then try it yourself.

Before you read beyond the next sentence, fill in the blanks. The two most important characteristics of effective business writing are: _____ and

_____.

No peeking. Don't read my list until you've found a pen or pencil and filled in the blanks. I want you to come to your own conclusions.

OK? Assignment completed?

Chances are you wrote "clear" and "concise." Am I right?

I've asked hundreds of business writers to do this exercise, and invariably they identify the same attributes. They also list a number of other characteristics – such as precise, specific, to the point, accurate, fast-paced, lively, energetic, interesting, forceful, enlightening, persuasive, informative, comprehensive, logical, and organized. But most describe effective business writing as clear and concise.

Clarity. It seems so simple and straightforward. Yet if clarity in business writing is such an obvious goal, why is it so elusive?

Well, for one thing, writing with clarity goes deeper than finding the right words to capture your thoughts. Clear writing is the result of clear thinking. As William Zinsser points out in *Writing To Learn,* "If you force yourself to think clearly, you will write clearly. It's as simple as that. The hard part isn't the writing; the hard part is the thinking."

To make the thinking part easier, try this exercise the next time you find yourself feeling lost when writing a report. Set aside your draft and complete this phrase in a simple, short sentence: The purpose of this report is _____. If you are thinking clearly, you should be able to define your main purpose in a simple, short sentence – even if you are writing a 1000-page report.

Once you've clarified your thinking (the hard part), you can begin to write clearly (the easy part). Clarity in writing is achieved on four levels: word choice, sentence structure, paragraph structure, and overall organization. Let's take these one by one.

■**Word choice.** To express yourself clearly, use language that is concise, unassuming, and appropriate to the audience. Strunk and White offer simple but sound advice in *The Elements of Style:* "Omit needless words." Furthermore, unless you have a good reason for using a fancy word, use a plain one.

■**Sentence structure.** Remember that short sentences are easier to follow than long sentences with complex structures. Often, the way to make sense of a confusing sentence is simply to cut it in two, particularly if you are in the habit of coupling your sentences with the conjunction and.

■**Paragraph structure.** The best advice here again comes from Strunk and White: Make the paragraph your basic unit of composition. If your paragraphs are well organized and carefully developed, your writing will probably be clear. Not every paragraph needs to be written according to the conventional three-part structure, but when you think you're in trouble, go back to the basics: topic sentence, development, resolution.

■**Overall organization.** You can also assure clarity by presenting your material in logical order. One way to check your organization is to make an outline of topic sentences from your paragraphs. If you have developed your argument logically, these statements should form a coherent progression in your thought.

Remember: According to your definition and mine, effective business writing is clear and concise. Not that these attributes are the only ones that matter. To paraphrase Beth Luey in *Handbook for Academic Authors,* if you can move beyond clarity to grace and elegance, you are to be congratulated. Your reader will happily settle, however, for clarity.

Writing Simply

Give readers a break – keep it plain and simple

Have you ever wondered why business writing often seems lifeless and dry? As though it were written by a machine rather than a human being?

Sometimes I think that when people write on the job they assume that they must use someone else's language, that being a professional requires them to resort to a kind of high-blown, unnatural language that is supposed to establish their prowess and their intelligence by its very obscurity and detachment. It's as though business writers are responsible to some higher authority that requires them to use phrases such as "As per your request" rather than "As you requested," or wording such as "It is my recommendation that we take action at the earliest possible time" rather than "I think we should take action immediately."

People who write this way fail to realize a simple truth about business writing: The reader wants to hear *their* voice, a human voice, not someone else's voice, and not some abstract construct of how business writing is supposed to sound.

If you want to connect with your reader, you should avoid language that seems stilted or unnecessarily formal in favor of language that sounds natural and genuine to your ear. Unless you have a good reason for choosing a fancy word, use a plain one.

Think of writing as a personal transaction between the writer and the reader. The words are the medium, merely the means of creating a relationship between you and your audience. The real subject is you – your thoughts, ideas, and values.

Let's take an example: "I deem it advisable that you and I should continue to interface in positive ways on this matter until such time as a solution can be found."

Admittedly, that's an extreme example of puffed-up, overdone, fancy language, but I would wager that you've probably come across something like it. (Some of you may even have *written* something like it – not to point any fingers.)

Now, does the language in that sentence give you a sense of the person behind the words? Perhaps more to the point, are you comfortable with that person? Do you like that person? Would you enjoy spending some time with that person?

Compare this version of the sentence: "I am eager to continue working with you to solve this problem."

Do you hear how this more natural language makes a better impression? A person who uses this kind of language seems more real, easier to be with, a more pleasant companion than someone who puffs up his or her thoughts with phony, inflated language.

So the next time you find yourself struggling over whether to use the word *commence* or *begin,* think of the golden rule of business writing: *Write unto others as you would have them write unto you.*

Remember: The secret to connecting with your reader is to be yourself, to use language that conveys a sense of your individuality, your humanity, and your warmth. It may take confidence to reveal who you are, but we really want to know. Don't hide behind your words.

Use language your readers know, expect

It is commonly said that there are three keys to effective writing: Know your audience, know your purpose, and know your material. If you have mastered these three keys, the words will flow more easily.

It's an excellent list. But I want to modify it somewhat and apply it to a particular type of writing that is critical to most businesses and agencies: writing to the customer. In my revised version, the three keys to writing to the customer are: Know your audience, know your audience, and know your audience.

Let's take these point by point. First, know your audience. This involves presenting yourself in a way that makes you seem like a real person – a human being, an individual with personality and character – rather than like a faceless bureaucrat.

The second key, knowing your audience, is even more important than the first. This entails having an ear for the language your audience is most comfortable with, and using that language in a natural and inviting way.

The third key, knowing your audience, is the most important of the three. In a very real sense, it is a product of the first two. This involves connecting with your audience by using language that reduces rather than increases the distance between you and your reader.

Unfortunately, choosing the plain word over the fancy one (as I advised you to do in my last column) may prove harder than it seems. The problem is that we tend to use certain phrases and expressions in our writing, not because they are the best, most natural and concise way to say what we have to say, but because we hear them frequently.

Like children learning bad grammar, we imitate bad usage because we get used to hearing it. The result is that we form bad habits, and, as everyone knows, bad habits are hard to break.

To help you get started breaking those habits, here's a

short list of commonly used expressions to avoid, as well as some suggestions for more natural, concise alternatives. I encourage you to keep this list on your writing desk or to tape it to your computer as a reminder. You might even want to add entries of your own.

EDIT THIS	TO THIS
deem	think
apprise	inform
ascertain	learn, find out
facilitate	help
commence	begin
finalize	end, settle, agree
transpire	happen
quantify	measure
cognizant of	aware of, aware that
desirous of	want
contingent upon	dependent on
until such time as	until
[as verbs]	
evidence	show
attempt	try
endeavor	try
impact	affect

Now, I know what some of you are thinking. The words on the left sound neater and glitzier than the ones on the right. Right? Asking you to give them up is like asking you to give up your Fruit Loops in the morning for a cereal that is low in sugar and high in fiber.

But go ahead. Try the plain variety. Like a wholesome cereal, it may not taste as good at first, but it will give you more energy and help you live longer in the end. See if the simpler, more natural language on the right doesn't make you feel better about yourself and doesn't fortify your sentences. It may even lower your reader's risk of heart failure.

How to avoid succumbing to acute prolixity

I want to take the opportunity of today's column to thank you, the reader, for your letters expressing your comments, questions, and concerns about business writing. It's heartening to discover that so many people recognize the importance of effective communication, and that so many of you care enough to express your views.

Most of the letters I have received have been very positive. Two readers, however, disagreed with my advice that, as a general rule, you should avoid fancy words in favor of simple, plain language.

The first person, a translator, pointed out that "Words high and words low have their uses in any language, a given reinforced by the fact that all words carry nuances of meaning." He warned that my approach "would lead, if inferred to its ultimate conclusion, to . . . illiteracy as a national standard and to our communicating by little more than grunts."

The second reader argued that "the effectiveness of 'fancy' words is the nuance and subtlety that they convey." He too worried that my advice contained a reductive element: "Mastering effective writing techniques at a sophisticated level is not easy, but the beauty of the language will certainly be lost with grunts, gestures, and facial expressions."

Both writers have a point. But both, I fear, missed mine.

Although I applaud those who would advocate for a wider expressive range in business writing, I also urge them caution. Watch out for language that obscures rather than elucidates your meaning. The number one attribute of effective business writing is clarity – plain and simple. For this reason, I would maintain that one well articulated grunt, clearly understood by the reader, is worth a thousand fuzzy words.

I wish I could claim to be the first writer in the history of the language to have recommended stylistic restraint. But it's common advice.

In their 1959 classic handbook, *The Elements of Style,*

Strunk and White offer advice directed specifically to the business writer when they warn against using "portentous nouns and verbs" that "at first glance seem freighted with delicious meaning but that soon burst in air, leaving nothing but a memory of bright sound." The same ideas, they point out, usually "can be expressed less formidably, if one wishes to do so."

In his 1976 book, *On Writing Well,* William Zinsser declares, "Clutter is the disease of American writing. We are a society strangling in unnecessary words, circular constructions, pompous frills and meaningless jargon."

According to Joseph Williams in his 1981 book, *Style: Ten Lessons in Clarity and Grace,* "There is a common word for almost every fancy borrowed one. When we pick the ordinary word we rarely lose anything important."

Twenty-two years ago, IBM Chairman Thomas J. Watson Jr. called for simpler language in a now-famous memo to his managers. "A foreign language has been creeping into many of the presentations I hear and the memos I read," he wrote. "It adds nothing to a message but noise. . . It's called gobbledygook."

To illustrate his point, he offered these examples: "Nothing seems to get finished anymore – it gets 'finalized.' Things don't happen at the same time but 'coincident with this action.' Believe it or not, people will talk about taking a 'commitment position' and then because of the 'volatility of schedule changes' they will 'decommit.'"

Finally, consider this. The column you are reading could be described in one of two ways. One might say, for example, that my purpose in writing this is to offer communication facilitation skills development intervention to linguistically determined and/or challenged individuals. Or, on the other hand, one might say that my purpose is to help people learn how to write more effectively on the job.

Which language do *you* prefer? It's your choice.

Writing Concisely

So many words, so strong the urge to "redunderize"

The Norman Conquest, beginning with the battle of Hastings in 1066, represents a pivotal development in the evolution of modern English. The defeat of King Harold of England at the hands of Duke William of Normandy and the subsequent rule by Norman nobles resulted in approximately 10,000 French words being assimilated into the English language. Of these, some 7,500 are still in use today.

This legacy gives us a language that is not only extraordinarily rich in quantity of words (the latest update of the American Heritage dictionary contains some 200,000 entries) but rich in synonyms (words and expressions that have the same or nearly the same meaning).

As Bill Bryson points out in *The Mother Tongue: English & How It Got that Way,* we English-speakers are presented with choices that many languages simply do not offer. We can choose, for example, to offer someone either "a hearty welcome" (which is derived from the old Anglo-Saxon words) or "a cordial reception" (which comes to us from Latin via French). The wording we choose depends on the tone and nuance that we desire.

To have such a plethora of choices is both a blessing and a curse. Synonyms have their uses, but availing ourselves of too many of these wonderful possibilities when expressing a simple thought can lead to a common problem in business writing: wordiness. (Or, if you prefer, prolixity, verbosity, loquaciousness, grandiloquence – see what I mean?)

In *Style: Ten Lessons in Clarity and Grace,* Joseph Williams cautions against three types of redundancy. The first is redundant modifiers (in which the modifier implies the meaning of the word modified, as in *past memories, personal beliefs, important essentials, consensus of opinion,* etc.). The second is redundant categories (in which the category is implied by the word, as in *large in size, pink in color, extreme in degree, honest in character,* etc.). The third is redundant pairs (in which the second word reiterates the meaning of the first, as in *first and foremost, hopes and desires, full and complete, precious and few,* and – if I may drop the italics – so on and so forth).

Redundant pairing, by the way, dates back (you guessed it!) to the Norman Conquest, when the disenfranchised Anglo-Saxons got in the habit of borrowing from the Norman nobles. As Williams explains, "Because the borrowed word usually sounded a bit more learned than the familiar native one, early writers would use both." So here we are, more than nine centuries later, still pairing our words – but then whoever said habits of speech were easy to break?

Despite our wonderful vocabulary, there are gaps in modern English. For example, we have no verb that corresponds to the adjective redundant. "Repeat," though close, is not precisely equivalent in meaning. We have only the more cumbersome phrase, "to be redundant."

To fill this gap, I would like to introduce a new word into English: "redunderize." I find it appealing for two reasons. First, its meaning is transparent to anyone who knows the meaning of "redundant." And second, it sounds like "dunderhead" – an apt description for a person who uses language in a redundant manner.

Now, here's an exercise to help you avoid being a dunderhead. See if you can unredunderize the following sentence into plain English: "Although at the present point in time high-speed rail is only now being evaluated in an accurate and timely fashion for the Twin Cities-Chicago shuttle, in the final analysis it is our hope and desire to ascertain once and for all whether or not passengers traveling this route in this day and age indeed have a decided and distinct preference for one of the several various and sundry transportation options and alternatives that will presently be available to them soon or in the near future." The unredunderized version might go like this: "High-speed rail is only now being evaluated as an option for the Twin Cities-Chicago shuttle."

You can also take a simple statement such as, "We need to finish the project on time," and redunderize it. Here's what I come up with: "I deem it absolutely and positively imperative and mandatory that we do our very best to completely finalize our work on this project in a timely and punctual fashion."

Get the idea? Now here's one for you to redunderize on your own: "We need to offer our customers good service." Go ahead. Have some fun with it. Let me know how you do.

Simple suggestions for simplifying sentences

"Clutter is the disease of American writing," William Zinsser declares in his book, *On Writing Well.* "We are a society strangling in unnecessary words, circular constructions, pompous frills, and meaningless jargon." The secret to good writing: "Strip every sentence to its cleanest components."

"Vigorous writing is concise," Strunk and White maintain in *The Elements of Style.* "A sentence should contain no unnecessary words, a paragraph no unnecessary sentences, for the same reason that a drawing should have no unnecessary lines and a machine no unnecessary parts." The goal for the writer: "Make every word tell."

Both books offer sound advice. But like so many things, stripping our writing of clutter is easier said than done.

The problem is that we are so overwhelmed with wordy expressions in everyday usage that we begin using these phrases without really hearing what we are saying or writing. Lost in a sea of "pompous frills and meaningless jargon," we sometimes forget that there are simpler, more direct ways of finding our way to shore.

Consider, for example, all the round-about ways of avoiding one the sturdiest, most useful words in the English language, *because.* These expressions include *on the grounds that, for the reason that, due to the fact that, based on the fact that, in view of the fact that,* and *owing to the fact that.* In place of any of these circumlocutions, a simple *because* will do.

Similarly, we hear phrases such as *in order to* and *for the purpose of* so often that we forget that we can simply write *to.* For example, instead of writing "*In order to* write clearly . . ." or "*For the purpose of* clear writing . . . ," we can get our sentence off to a faster, more vigorous start by simply writing, "*To* write clearly, use simple language."

Likewise, you might catch yourself using *in the event that* when all you mean is *if,* as in "*In the event that* you have any questions . . ." rather than the simpler, more direct "*If* you have any questions, please contact me."

Now, just for fun, let's illustrate the effect of wordiness by stringing together a series of commonly used, wordy expressions and then editing them into more concise language. Here's a memo that needs stripping:

"We are in receipt of your shipment in the amount of 250 Concise Writing Computer Chips. In view of the fact that the shipment arrived one year late, however, we have no other choice but to return it.

"During the course of the past year, our employees, with the possible exception of our vice president, have learned to eliminate wordy language from the writing they do on a daily basis. Until such time as we decide the question as to whether or not computer assistance is needed, I can't help but think we will rely on more conventional methods."

I'll make the editing easy. Take your pen or pencil and cross out the wordier expression in each pairing below:

"We [are in receipt of / received] your shipment [in the amount of / of] 250 Concise Writing Computer Chips. [In view of the fact that / Because] the shipment arrived one year late, however, we [have no other choice but to / must] return it.

"[During the course of / During] the past year, our employees, [with the possible exception of / except] our vice president, have learned to eliminate wordy language from [the writing they do on a daily basis / their daily writing]. [Until such time as / Until] we decide [the question as to whether or not / whether] computer assistance is needed, I [can't help but think / think] we will rely on more conventional methods."

Hear the difference? Do you agree that the more concise version is also the more vigorous? The lesson is simple: Watch out for wordiness. There's a lot of it going around these days, and it's catching.

How to write ambiguously to cover your amphibology

As we have been discussing in the past few columns, good business writing is, above all, clear and concise. Right?

Right. Well . . . at least most of the time.

But let's be honest. Haven't you, at least once or twice in your professional career, found yourself withholding information, presenting incomplete data, or being deliberately vague? Perhaps "distortion" is too strong a word. Let's call it "shaping" the facts into evidence that best supports your argument or point of view.

We all do it. Whether this practice amounts to deception or persuasion depends, I suppose, on degree and intent. But the point is that, at least on some occasions, good business writing doesn't tell the whole story. It isn't meant to. Sometimes it is deliberately unclear. It gives only the illusion of clarity.

To be more accurate, then, we should say that good business writing is, as a rule, clear and concise but, on occasion, intentionally ambiguous. And to carry this a step further, let's distinguish between intentional ambiguity (which is sometimes acceptable and necessary) and unintentional ambiguity (which is nearly always unacceptable and avoidable). Which takes us back to clarity.

Assuming for now that intentional ambiguity comes pretty naturally to most of us, let's concentrate on four types of unintentional ambiguity: ambiguous pronoun reference, misplaced and dangling modifiers, squinting modifiers, and – my favorite – amphibologies (which can be either intentional or unintentional).

■**Ambiguous pronoun reference.** A pronoun is a word such as *he, she,* or *it* that takes the place of a noun. To avoid ambiguity, the noun to which a pronoun refers must be clear. For example, in this sentence, "Mary told Susan that her proposal was approved by the board," the pronoun *her* could refer either to Mary or to Susan. One way to eliminate the ambiguity here is to repeat the noun: "Mary told Susan that

Susan's proposal was approved by the board."

■**Misplaced and dangling modifiers.** As their names imply, misplaced and dangling modifiers cause confusion (often with ludicrous results) because they are placed too far from the words they modify. Sometimes, misplaced modifiers come at the end of a sentence, as in: "Our products are shipped by our clerks wrapped attractively in decorative paper." More often, however, misplaced modifiers come at the beginning of the sentence: "When completely plastered, you need to start painting the walls" and "Although loud-mouthed and pushy, I think we owe this customer an apology." To correct this problem, place the words that the introductory phrases actually modify – *the walls* and *this customer* – *immediately* after the comma, as in "Although loud-mouthed and pushy, this customer deserves an apology."

■**Squinting modifiers.** This type of modifier causes ambiguity because it "squints" or "looks in two directions at once." In the sentence, "Writing clearly is hard work," the adverb *clearly* could be understood to modify both *writing* and *is.* Does the sentence mean "Clear writing is hard work" or "It is clear that writing is hard work"?

■**Amphibologies.** And now for the fun one. Amphibologies are phrases or sentences that have two, often contrary meanings. For example, consider the meaning of this notice on a receptionist's desk: "If you think I'm rude, you should see my manager." Or how about this well-intentioned but regrettable sentence in a performance appraisal: "I can't say too many good things about Sam's leadership"?

Certain unusually gifted writers have made amphibolic writing into an art, such as former British Prime Minister Benjamin Disraeli, who once responded to an aspiring author: "Thank you so much for the book. I shall lose no time in reading it."

If you can do better than that one, I'd like to hear from you.

Writing Correctly

Using parallel structure honors contract with reader

If Benjamin Franklin had written, "Early to bed, early to rise, makes a man healthy, wealthy, and a C.E.O.," we wouldn't be quoting him today.

Instead, he began his list with two adjectives, *healthy* and *wealthy,* and completed it not with a noun, *C.E.O.,* but with a third adjective, *wise,* thereby rendering his maxim memorable. What he did was follow parallel structure, a technique that lends a sentence rhythm and cadence. It not only sounds good; it creates emphasis.

The principle of parallel structure is a simple one. Plainly put, the reader expects consistency. Ideas that are related to each other (grammarians like to call these "coordinate" ideas) should be expressed in parallel form. Expressions similar in content and function should be expressed similarly.

Here's how it works.

If you begin making a list with adjectives, as Ben did, you enter a contract with the reader to complete your list in like fashion. If you switch to a different part of speech somewhere in your list, you break the contract and jar the reader.

The point is to be consistent. Create an expectation in your reader's mind, and then meet that expectation. It's a nice trick. It makes the reader think that you know what you're doing, that you're in the driver's seat, that you're in control.

Get the idea? Here's a sentence with nonparallel structure: "She is capable, experienced, and often works late at night."

Doesn't sound right, does it? In this sentence the writer breaks the contract with the reader by shifting from a series of adjectives, *capable* and *experienced,* to a verb phrase, *often works late at night.*

The result is a break in rhythm, a loss of momentum. To honor the contract, the writer should have written, "She is capable, experienced, and dedicated" – or "talented" or "brilliant" or whatever adjective came to mind, as long as it was another adjective.

If on the other hand the writer was partial to the verb phrase, liked the sound of it and didn't want to give it up, the sentence could have been rewritten this way: "A capable and dedicated employee, she often works until late at night."

Either way, the writer avoids one of the most common errors in business writing, the sentence is vastly improved, and the reader doesn't feel cheated.

Here's another example: "The volume of business depends on an institution's delivery method, production time, and whether or not it is open or closed."

Can you hear where the sentence violates parallel structure and loses its momentum? To eliminate the breach in contract, the series should be concluded as it was begun – with a third noun phrase, like this: "delivery method, production time, and hours of operation."

Remember: The point is to be consistent.

Now, here's one for you to correct on your own: "Either finish the project on time or I think you need to ask me for help." Can you hear how the unnecessary phrase breaks the momentum of the sentence?

To make sure you're following parallel structure in your own writing, you need to do more than just read about it; you need to practice using it. To help you do this, I'm going to give you an assignment.

I know. That's unfair. There you are, sipping coffee over your morning paper, trying to relax a little before going to work, and someone has the nerve to give you an assignment. Well, I'm sorry, but it's for your own good.

Here it is: Look for breakdowns in parallel structure in everything that you read or write during the next week. Mark the problems you find with your pen or yellow marker. Then practice correcting them.

OK? Let me know if you have any questions or if you come across any especially interesting examples.

How to proofread and never miss a single errror

We all have horror stories we can tell about proofreading errors, about those times when, despite our best efforts, something slipped past our vigilant gaze.

Sometimes these lapses are relatively harmless. Other times, if we're lucky, our readers don't even notice. All too often, however, the errors are obvious and painfully embarassing.

Four years ago this May, for example, the University of Wisconsin awarded nearly 4,000 diplomas with the name of the state spelled *Wisconson.* Amazingly, six months passed before anyone noticed and brought it to the University's attention. "We do proofread the diplomas," said one official, "but we concentrate on the name and the degree. We usually consider that the standard information is correct. It just didn't occur to us that this could happen." But it did happen, and the printing company ended up paying for replacements.

Once during my days as an administrator at the University of Minnesota I was serving on a search committee. Of the more than 130 applications, one stood out. The application letter began with a reference to the position of "associate vice president for student affairs at the University of Minnesota" and concluded with a statement about "the real reason I want to come to the University of Maryland is . . ." The committee members recognized the gaffe as a word-processing error, an illustration of both the power and the risk of electronically produced text, and we had a good chuckle. Needless to say, however, the applicant didn't get the job.

In fairness to word processors, it must be acknowledged that these wonderful machines and their marvelous spell-checking programs have led to a dramatic reduction in mispellings. No longer is it commonplace, for example, to see *accommodate* spelled with one *m, commitment* spelled with a double *t* after the *i,* or that formerly much-abused word, *occurrence,* misspelled three different ways in a single attempt:

with one *c*, one *r*, and an *a* rather than an *e*. But even the wizardry of computers won't prevent you from using the wrong word, correctly spelled – such as *effect* when you mean *affect*, or *complement* when you mean *compliment*.

In other words, affective proofreading is still an important and necessary skill. To help you sharpen that skill, I recommend the following techniques:

1. Read slowly and fixate on each word.
2. Sub – vocalize (or, better yet, read out loud).
3. Read one line at a time (try holding a ruler or sheet of paper beneath each line as you read it).
4. When you find an error, reread the entire sentence (for some reason, we tend to assume that a sentence will have no more than one error).
5. Check for consistency in format (in headings, spacing, punctuation, layout, etc.)
7. Watch for common errors (such as *it's* for *its,* or missing quotation marks and parentheses – especially the closing marks.
8. Pay special attention to headings (their authoritative appearance can fool you).
9. Check not only for typographical errors but for common word-processing errors such as repeated, missing, repeated, and misplaced text.
10. Have someone who was not involved in the preparation of your text check it over.
11. Because certain errors can be caught more readily by the author, be sure to proofread your own copy when someone else is doing your typing.
12. Finally – as recommended in 1978 by the National Secretaries Association – proofread tomorrow what you worked on today.

Now, as you have doubtless noticed, this column is studded with errors. I did this intentionally to give you some practice applying the proofreading techniques I am recommending. Not counting *Wisconson* for *Wisconsin,* there are nine – at least, I think that's how many there are. (Let me know if you find more!) Can you find all nine? Work with a colleague if you like. Answers will appear in next weeks column.

Happy hunting!

How did you do on my proofreading quiz?

In my previous column, I offered 11 techniques for foolproof proofreading. On the assumption that people learn more effectively when given the opportunity to apply the knowledge and skills they are being taught, I included a number of intentional errors in my copy – nine, to be exact – and I invited you to find them.

How did you do? Did get help from a colleague?

Most of the errors were obvious, but some may have been hard to spot. At least one was inconspicuous. I suspect that only the most skilled proofreaders among you found all nine.

Here are the errors as they appeared, beginning with the misspelling in the headline.

Error 1: How to proofread and never miss a single errror

That's an easy one. *Errror* should have a double rather than a triple *r*.

Error 2: "All too often, however, the errors are obvious and painfully embarassing."

For some odd reason, *embarrass* is correctly spelled with a double *r,* whereas *harass* is spelled with a single *r*. Inconsistencies of this nature were slipped into the English language by unscrupulous lexicographers for the sole purpose of making life difficult for the rest of us. If you've ever met an lexicographer, you know how diabolical they can be.

Error 3: "In fairness to the word processor, however, it must be acknowledged that these wonderful machines and their marvelous spell-checking programs have led to a dramatic reduction in mispellings."

I'm embarrassed by this one. I can't believe my spell-checker didn't catch it for me. As I'm sure you noticed, *mispellings* should be spelled *misspellings*. I confess: spelling will always be a mystery to me. And here I was preaching to you about the importance of getting it write.

Error 4: "In other words, affective proofreading is still an important and necessary skill."

There's another one! That should be *effective,* which means producing a decisive or desired effect, as opposed to *affective,* which means relating to feelings or emotions. If you have trouble knowing when to use *affect* or *effect,* just memorize this phrase (and note that the two words are in alphabetical order): To *a*ffect something, you must have an *e*ffect on it. Remember: *Affect* is almost always used as a verb; *effect* is almost always used as a noun. The only common usage for *effect* as a verb is in this phrase: *to effect change.* Otherwise, if you're looking for a verb, the safe bet is *affect.*

Errors 5, 6, & 7:

"5. Check for consistency in format (in headings, spacing, punctuation, layout, etc.)

7. Watch for common errors (such as *it's* for *its,* or missing quotation marks and parentheses – especially the closing marks."

There are three errors contained in these two points of advice. If you found the first one, which is hardly noticeable, you are to be commended as a very fine proofreader indeed: Item 5 is the only item in the list that does not end with a period. In addition, the numbering is faulty (number 6 is skipped), and item 7 is missing its closing parenthesis.

Error 8: "Check not only for typographical errors but for common word-processing errors such as repeated, missing, repeated, and misplaced text."

Ah, the electronic gremlin strikes again, leaving a chunk of *repeated* text where it doesn't belong.

Error 9: "Answers will appear in next weeks column."

Watch out for apostrophes when forming the possessive. They are easily omitted. In this case, an apostrophe is needed to form the possessive of *week,* as in *next week's column.*

Well, I hope this little exercise wasn't too painful for you. But who ever said writing was supposed to be fun, anyway?

By the way, if you want to share any of your favorite horror stories about proofreading errors, I'd love to hear them. You'll find me at www.wilbers.com.

"Porn and Beans" and other proofreading classics

Well, I can see we need another column on proofreading errors.

My columns on proofreading elicited three times the number of letters that my columns typically generate. (Thanks, Mom, Dad, Sis.)

Responding to my invitation to share favorite horror stories about proofreading, Colleen Hofelman of Pipestone wrote that her local grocery store was offering a real attention-grabber as its special of the week: "Porn and Beans."

Which reminds me of the one my editor shared with me from the headline in a Catholic weekly newspaper: "The joy of pubic worship."

Philip Carlson, a Minneapolis landscape architect, sent in this one: "My biggest blooper was in a letter to an important out-of-town client. I typed the letter and studied the body of it carefully for errors, including spell-checking in the computer. Only after I had sent it did I notice I had addressed it to 'Mr. *Brain* (instead of Brian) Brennan.' If he noticed, he never told me."

Jane Perkins from Mankato thinks that the typo in Jane Smiley's Pulitzer prize-winning novel, *A Thousand Acres,* "should win the big one!" On page 294, *eulogy* is misspelled *eulegy,* but Ms. Perkins "almost" likes it that way because, she notes, *eulegy* could be "a combination of *eulogy* and *elegy.*"

And then there was the one from Irene Bohn, of New Hope Elementary School, who wrote about the two grown men who went out, with dogs and rifles in tow, to do some "mouse hunting."

The story that best illustrates how costly proofreading errors can be came from Winifred Lanches of Richfield (who, by the way, was relieved when she read in the last paragraph of my column that I had made all those errors intentionally – until that point, she told me, she "was beginning to wonder" how I had "made it as a columnist!"). Ms. Lanches shared an anecdote "from many years ago" about a traveling sales rep of a large produce company who wired his boss one day to find out if he should accept the price he had been quoted for a quantity of produce. The boss called Western Union to send a wire, which read: "NO PRICE TOO HIGH." With this in mind, the sales rep bought an entire carload, only to learn on his return that what the boss had intended to say was: "NO. PRICE TOO HIGH."

Ah, so much for the price of a missing period! Or should that be "cost"?

Some of you wrote to describe particular proofreading "afflictions." As a member of a newspaper family, Charles Dare of Elk River has been proofreading all his life. In fact, even in retirement Mr. Dare is still so "afflicted" with "proofreading compulsion" that he proofs everything he reads, even signs and notices, and when he thinks he spots an error he calls the company.

Stella Waletski of Anoka had another kind of affliction in mind when she wrote, "Do you have any idea what it is like to live for years with a live, breathing, walking dictionary?" She was referring, of course, to her husband.

A number of readers, including B.J. Gades of Morris and Lucy Bigelow Hazel of St. Cloud, wrote to inform me that they had found an "unintended" error in my sentence, "And here I was preaching to you about the importance of getting it write." Ms. Hazel rote, "By the way, sir, your computer didn't do 'write' by you and neither did your proofreader."

Right. "Write" should indeed be "right" in the phrase, "getting it write." But which of these is right: Does a playwright write or does a playwrite wright?

And, if that's too easy for you, try this: How many rites could a playwright write if a playwright could write right? Or, if you prefer: How many wrongs could a playwright right if a playwright could right wrongs? Or should that be "writes"?

Keep those letters coming!

RULES, Rules, and rules:
How to tell them apart

Have you ever had the feeling that the people who devised the rules of English grammar did so for the diabolical purpose of making you look bad?

Well, you're not far from the truth.

Even the knowledgeable E. B. White, co-author of the classic writing handbook, *The Elements of Style,* recognized the complexity and capriciousness of the rules that govern our language when he wrote, "English usage is sometimes more than mere taste, judgment, and education – sometimes it's sheer luck, like getting across the street."

To make matters worse, no sooner do we learn a few rules and begin to think we know how to apply them then someone tells us they have changed. *Is that fair?* It's like trying to hit a moving target.

Let's see if I can bring some order to the chaos.

First of all, it's helpful to keep in mind that not all rules were created equal. That's right. As Joseph Williams points out in *Style: Ten Lessons in Clarity & Grace,* many rules have come to us as a consequence of "largely random accumulation" and "not all rules of usage have equal standing with all writers of English, even all careful writers of English."

To prevent these edicts from getting the better of us, let's divide them into three categories: There are *RULES* that you should always observe because they have won almost universal acceptance. There are *Rules* that you should sometimes observe, depending on your audience and your intended stylistic effect. And there are *rules* that simply aren't worth observing.

Here are examples of each.

RULES:

These are the *RULES* known to every educated writer: Don't use double negatives, verbs must agree with their subjects, avoid double comparatives, etc.

Other examples in this category are *RULES* that *should* be known to every educated writer but sometimes are not: the difference between *it's* and *its* (*it's* is a contraction of *it is; its* is the possessive pronoun), or the correct use of the reflexive pronoun (used when the subject of the sentence acts upon itself, as in "I hurt myself"; not when a pronoun is used as a subject or object, as in "Jane and myself [should be *I*] will attend the meeting" or "You can give the report to either John or myself [should be *me*]").

Rules:

These are *Rules* that you may choose to follow or to ignore, depending on the occasion and your intent. For example, as a general rule a paragraph should have more than one sentence to allow for adequate development. But you may choose to write a one-sentence paragraph for special emphasis. Likewise, as a matter of practice you should express your thought in complete sentences (groups of words that contain subjects and predicates and are not introduced by subordinating conjunctions). But you may choose to use a sentence fragment for special effect. Like this.

Keep in mind, however, that when you choose to ignore these *Rules,* you always pay a price with certain readers who expect you to follow them inflexibly.

rules:

I like this category the best. If you think about it, knowing that certain *rules* are not worth observing frees you from a good deal of nonsense. It empowers you as a writer.

As evidenced by the practice of many careful writers, you may freely ignore the following: Never split an infinitive. Never begin a sentence with *because.* Never begin a sentence with *and* or *but.* And never end a sentence with a preposition.

Perhaps Winston Churchill said it best when someone chided him for breaking the preposition rule: "This is the sort of arrant pedantry up with which I will not put."

And neither should you.

Between you and I, us writers should know better

For the past several years I have tried (with limited success) to get my son to stop saying, "Me and Andy are going down to the creek."

"Eddie," I tell him. "It's not '*Me* and Andy.' It's 'Andy and *I*.' 'Andy and *I* are going down to the creek.'"

I know what you're thinking. Poor kid. It must be tough growing up with an English-major father constantly correcting your grammar.

So let me set the record straight. I don't critique every word my son speaks or writes. Honest. But when it comes to something as basic and simple as pronoun case, I want him to get it right. You know: Teach children the basics, and they can avoid making certain mistakes all their adult lives. That sort of thing.

"O.K.," he says, with that winsome smile of his. "Will you take Andy and *I* down to the creek?"

"No," I tell him. "It's not 'Andy and *I*.' It's 'Andy and *me*.' 'Will you take Andy and *me* down to the creek?'"

"Dad!" he cries in exasperation. "You're changing the rules!"

Well, it must seem that way – not only to my 13-year-old son but also to millions of adult Americans (businesspeople included) who never quite got those pronouns straight when they were growing up.

Here's how they work.

Pronouns come in eight varieties: personal *(I, you, he, she, it, we,* and *they),* demonstrative *(this, these; that, those),* relative *(who or whom, which,* and *that),* interrogative *(who* or *whom, what,* and *which),* indefinite (*all, any, another, anyone, anything,* etc.), reflexive *(myself, yourself, himself, herself, itself, oneself, ourselves, yourselves,* and *themselves),* intensive (identical in form to reflexive), and reciprocal *(one another* and *each other).*

Certain pronouns take different forms according to their

use or case. In English, pronouns have three cases: subjective (or nominative), objective (or accusative), and possessive (or genitive). (If you're beginning to feel sorry for yourself, just remember that Latin has *five* cases for its pronouns, so things could be worse.)

When pronouns are used as the *subject* of a clause or sentence (I'll let you fill in the blanks), they take the _____ case. When used as the *object* of a verb or a preposition, they take the _____ case. And when used to express *ownership,* they take the _____ case.

Usually, the correct use of the subjective and objective case is obvious: *"I* called *her"* – not *"Her* called *I."* The possessive case is equally obvious: "Is this report *yours?"* – not "Is this report *you?"*

Easy enough.

Pronoun errors in business writing commonly occur, however, when the pronoun is used in combination with a noun, as in these three instances:

■Using the subjective rather than the objective case after a preposition, as in "between you and *I* [should be *me*]" or "Send the memo to Kathy and *I"* [should be *me*].

■Incorrectly substituting the reflexive for the personal pronoun, as in "George, Jane, and *myself* will attend" [should be *I*] or "Send the memo to Kathy and *myself"* [should be *me*].

■Mistaking the case of a pronoun when it is followed immediately by a noun, as in *"Us* writers never make mistakes [should be *we*] or "He addressed his remarks to *we* executives [should be *us*]."

The way to guard against these errors is easy: Try the sentence without the noun, as in "Send the memo to *me*" or *"We* never make mistakes."

Why do we make these errors? In *A Treasury for Word Lovers,* Morton S. Freeman theorizes that perhaps "to the untutored mind *between you and I* has to be correct because it sounds as though it ought to be."

So, watch out for these common pronominal errors. Meanwhile, I'll keep on tutoring my son, my daughter, and my associates. You do the same. Even one untutored mind is one too many.

Parts of speech lost on unsuspecting writer

The other day I saw a man standing on a street corner. He was patting the pockets of his trench coat and casting desperate glances at the sidewalk around him. Rarely have I seen someone so obviously distraught.

"Excuse me, sir," I said, walking up to him. "Have you lost something? Can I help you?"

He looked at me as though I were an angel sent from heaven.

"Yes. Please!" he said with tears coming to his eyes. "I keep misplacing my modifiers. I can't find them anywhere. Every time I open my mouth to speak or I sit down to write, I lose one. It's embarrassing. It's humiliating. No one at work will take me seriously."

"There, there," I said. "Calm down. You'll be just fine."

In my many years as a teacher and writing consultant, I've seen some bad cases of misplaced modifiers, but never anything like this.

"Here. Take two of these," I said, pulling from my briefcase copies of Strunk and White's *The Elements of Style* and Dornan and Dawe's *The Brief English Handbook.* "Get a good night's sleep and come see me in my office at nine o'clock tomorrow morning."

The next day he was standing outside my door when I arrived.

He looked at me through swollen, bloodshot eyes.

"Did you sleep well?" I asked.

"No," he replied. "I stayed up all night reading those books you gave me. I finished them both."

"You read both books?"

"Yes. Six times each."

"And did they help?"

"Well, I thought so. But then I caught myself saying, 'When pickled, I think herring tastes like caviar' and 'If well oiled, I find it easier to open my door.'"

"Hmmmm," I said, inviting him in. "This could be serious. Better have a look. Show me some more sentences."

He handed me a sheet of paper. There, covering the entire page, were sentences with their modifying elements nowhere near the words they modified.

"Well, I think I can help you," I said.

"You can?" he asked eagerly.

"Yes. Just follow this simple rule. Because English depends heavily on word order for meaning, place your related words as close as possible to one another.

"Look here," I said, pointing to a sentence that read, 'Walking down the corridor, the fax machine bumped into me.' Who is doing the walking here? *You* are, not the fax machine. So after the comma, the next word must be *I.* 'Walking down the corridor, *I* bumped into the fax machine.'

"Here's another one: 'The defendant was arrested for fornicating under a little-used statute.' That last phrase tells you *how* he was arrested, not where he committed the act. So move the phrase closer to the verb 'arrested,' like this: 'The defendant was arrested under a little-used statute for fornicating.' Get the idea?"

He nodded eagerly.

"Remember: Keep your related words close to each other and you'll be just fine."

He seemed satisfied, but later that afternoon I got a desperate call.

"Can you come over?" he blurted. "Right away? I've found all those misplaced modifiers, but now I've got another problem. I better warn you: It's bad."

When I walked into his office, I was shocked by what I saw. Hanging like leeches from his tile ceiling and light fixture were thousands of participial, infinitive, and prepositional phrases as well as hundreds of elliptical clauses, many of them introduced by *-ing* words and followed by passive constructions. It was not a pretty sight.

"This *is* serious," I agreed, realizing that I would need another column on the subject. "What you've got here is a bad case of dangling modifiers."

To be continued in my next column . . .

Curing twin diseases: Misplaced & dangling modifiers

Last week, I met a man who was suffering from a serious case of misplaced modifiers. We spent the better part of a morning reattaching modifying phrases to the words they modified, until at last he declared himself healed.

Later that afternoon, however, he called and pleaded with me to come to his office. What I saw was not pretty.

Hanging like leeches from his tile ceiling and light fixture were thousands of participial, infinitive, and prepositional phrases. It was a classic case. Cured of misplacing his modifiers, he had fallen prey to its twin disease: *dangling* modifiers.

"Will I be all right, Doc?" he said. "I never was any good at English. I don't even know what a participial phrase is, much less a dangling modifier. In seventh grade English we threw spitballs at the teacher. We were so disruptive that she resigned midway through the year." His voice dropped to a hoarse whisper. "I never dreamed it would come to this."

"Now, now," I said. "This is no time for confessions. Don't worry about the terminology. Just make sure those modifying phrases are near the words they modify, and you'll be fine. Let's get to work."

I took off my jacket, rolled up my sleeves, and – because dangling modifiers are such highly contagious constructions – pulled on my latex gloves.

"Let's start with that one," I said, pointing to a particularly nasty-looking strain hanging from the light fixture.

I grasped it firmly (dangling modifiers can be slippery) and gave it a tug. It came loose with a little *smack*.

"Looks like Strain A: a dangling participial phrase. Where's the rest of the sentence?"

He pointed to the main clause, which lay in a tangled heap of sentences on his desk. I pulled it loose and held it next to the dangling phrase.

"Here's the problem," I said. "Look at this sentence:

'Writing without stopping, the report was finished by noon.' Can you see what's wrong?"

"Well, yes," he said. "The sentence doesn't make sense."

"That's right. Why doesn't it?"

"Because the *report* didn't do the writing. *I* did the writing."

"And where are *you* in the sentence?"

"I don't know. I guess I forgot to put myself in there."

"Precisely. Your sentence is missing a 'doer.' To avoid dangling your introductory phrase, 'Writing without stopping,' you need to make sure that your main clause begins with the 'doer,' like this: 'Writing without stopping, *I* finished the report by noon.' Do you see the difference?"

He buried his face in his hands and groaned, "Oh, why did we throw those spitballs? She was only trying to help us."

"Come on, now. You can do it." I reached up and plucked another phrase from the ceiling.

"Now, here's an example of Strain B: a dangling infinitive phrase. *You* fix this one: 'To improve your writing skills, practice is needed.'"

He quickly supplied the missing "doer": "To improve your writing skills, *you* need to practice."

"Excellent. Now for Strain C: a dangling prepositional phrase."

I found one and held it out for him: "After asking for a raise, my boss told me to work harder."

"'After asking for a raise, *I* was told by my boss to work harder.'"

"Correct. But you can make the sentence shorter and more direct by placing the 'doer' in the first part."

"Do you mean like this? 'After *I* asked for a raise, my boss told me to work harder.'"

"Exactly."

"Wow!" he said. "Thanks, Doc! How can I ever repay you?"

I handed him my bill. It was all in a day's work.

I went home feeling particularly satisfied with my life as a writing consultant. That night I dreamed of reattaching millions of dangling modifiers to their missing "doers."

Ah, life is sweet.

Writing with Emphasis

You can take those important words and park 'em

A friend of mine who works for a major airline confided to me one day that the some of his supervisors write so poorly that the hourly workers have taken to correcting their memos in red ink and posting the results on bulletin boards for all to see.

"It's funny," he said. "But it's also sad. It's embarrassing. They're our bosses. We expect them to know better."

Many people in many professions have encountered similar situations: The people they look to for leadership and inspiration often don't write well. And because these leaders lack the basic skills needed to express their ideas and opinions convincingly, their credibility suffers.

To help you avoid being one of those unfortunate people whose writing is a source of embarrassment – both to you and to your company – I am offering simple, easy-to-apply advice on how to write effectively on the job.

Today's lesson is a technique for writing with greater emphasis.

The secret of this technique is knowing where the natural stress falls in a sentence, and making sure that your important words occupy that position. The principle is that certain locations in a sentence count more than others, just as certain parking places cost more than others.

Whether poetry or prose, the rule is the same: The first and last words of a line or sentence carry more weight than the words in the middle. And the word that carries the most weight of all is the one that comes last.

I like to call that final position "V.I.P. Parking." Only very important words can park there.

As you begin to look over and revise what you have written, think of each sentence as an assemblage of moveable parts. A writer concerned with emphasis takes care to shift those parts around so that the most significant ones come at the sentence's beginning or end and are not buried in the middle.

You can check the validity of this principle with your own

ear. Take this sentence as an example: "The study suggests that we could increase sales by at least 15% if we adopted the marketing technique employed by the XYZ Company."

Read it out loud so you can really hear it.

Now, let's assume that you consider the idea of the *marketing technique* more significant here than the name of the company that is using it. To reflect that emphasis, try rearranging the sentence so that the more important phrase, *marketing technique,* falls at the end, like this: "The study suggests that we could increase sales by at least 15% if we adopted XYZ Company's marketing technique."

Now read that version out loud. Can you hear the difference in emphasis?

If, on the other hand, you're a bottom-line kind of person, you may prefer this version: "The study suggests that, if we adopted XYZ Company's marketing technique, we could increase sales by at least 15%." Can you hear the new emphasis?

The choice is yours. The principle is the same. Reserve that V.I.P. slot for your most important words and you will write with more energy and vigor.

Well, there you have the secret to writing with emphasis – or at least one of the secrets anyway. Try it and see if it doesn't make a difference.

Now. One last item. If any of you are looking for examples of missed emphasis in this column with the intent of posting the corrected copy on the bulletin board and embarrassing me, forget it. It won't work. I can always claim I was just fooling around.

When sentences ramble, just cut the engine

Sometimes, in writing as in life, we just don't know when to stop. And when we let our sentences ramble on for a few words more than needed, we miss an important opportunity to present our thoughts with emphasis and conviction.

I like to compare this to turning off my engine on a cold January morning in Minnesota. My car has done its work. It has taken me to my destination. But when I switch off the ignition, my engine sometimes diesels – goes *putt, putt, putt* – before it finally quits.

Sometimes your sentences do the same thing. Even after they have taken you to your destination and nothing more is needed, they go *putt, putt, putt* for a few more words. If you want to write with emphasis and energy, you need to learn how to cut them off, make them stop, neatly and cleanly, when the job is done. As author Joseph Williams and others have pointed out, the trick to managing the emphasis of your sentences is often a matter of merely trimming off the endings.

In my previous column I explained an important technique for writing with greater emphasis: placing your most important words at the end of your sentences, where the natural stress falls. As you may recall, I like to think of that final, privileged position as "V.I.P. Parking" because only very important words can park there.

And I suggested that one way you can play to your sentence's natural stress is by rearranging the order of your words and phrases.

In this column I want to recommend a second method for ensuring that the important words fall in that special parking place. On those occasions when your engine sputters, gasps, and wheezes for a few words more than are strictly necessary, simply lop off the ending.

Take this sentence as an illustration: "We need to do something now about the problems we are experiencing." Pretty lackluster and dull, wouldn't you say?

Here's how to fix it. First, decide which is the more important word: *problems* or *experiencing*? Well, obviously, the main thought of the sentence has to do with *problems*. Can you hear how the sentence goes *putt, putt, putt* beyond its real destination?

Now, trim the phrase *we are experiencing* and listen to the way the natural stress of the sentence reinforces and underscores the main point: "We need to do something now about these problems." Or better yet: "We need to do something about these problems now." Once you are in command of your sentence, you can make the stress fall on almost any word you like.

One practical way to apply the "V.I.P. Parking" principle to the writing you do on the job is to watch for that ever-popular phrase *as follows*. It's a washout, a piece of fluff. Whenever you find yourself using it with a colon to introduce a list of items, try trimming it off.

For example, "My goals for this project are as follows: . . ." has more emphasis and energy if written, "My goals for this project are: . . ." The phrase "as follows" is unnecessary and can almost always be eliminated.

You can also apply this principle of natural stress to paragraphs, where the first and last sentences carry more weight than do the sentences in the middle. (In a conventional paragraph, these are the topic sentence and the conclusion.) Likewise, the first and last paragraphs in a report are more important – in fact are read more frequently and with greater care – than the paragraphs in the middle.

The lesson in each case is obvious: Try to position your most important words at the beginning and the end of each sentence, your most important sentences at the beginning and the end of each paragraph, and your most important paragraphs at the beginning and the end of each document.

To help you remember today's lesson in V.I.P. Parking and knowing when to turn off your engine, I'd like to leave you with this quote from William Zinsser: "There's not much to be said about the period except that most writers don't reach it soon enough."

Now, that's something to think about, isn't it?

Character, action essential to livening up prose

One of the best ways to keep your readers' attention is by telling stories. That's right. You can add life to even the dullest communication by presenting your information in narrative form. The principle here is a simple one: Readers like stories.

Here's how it works. Whenever possible, make sure that your sentences contain the two essential ingredients of every story: character and action.

Think about it. You can't have a story without these two elements – even if you're Franz Kafka writing about a man who wakes up one morning and discovers, much to his chagrin, that he has turned into a cockroach.

When sentences fail to tell a story, the writing is often lifeless and dull. We sometimes call this type of writing "bureaucratese" or "business jargon." Whatever we call it, the point is that nobody really wants to read it.

As writing consultant Sherry Sweetnam explains in *The Executive Memo,* not only is this type of writing worn-out and boring, but it "heightens the problem of people feeling dehumanized because it's boilerplated and not authentic. People want words that reflect a real person, not a cold, vacant writer."

The way to avoid lifeless writing is to express your thought whenever possible in terms of characters taking actions. That makes it a story. And remember: People like stories.

Compare, for example, the following phrases. In the left column are dull, lifeless expressions devoid of human action or activity. On the right are more interesting ways of conveying the same information by using character and action:

As per your order	As you ordered
As per our conversation	As we discussed
In accordance with your request	As you requested
Pursuant to our agreement	We agreed that
The purpose of this letter is to	I am writing to you to

Now, admittedly the acts of ordering, discussing, requesting, agreeing, and writing may not be the most exciting actions known to humankind – nothing as dramatic as, say, Oedipus Rex gouging out his eyes when he discovers that he has unwittingly murdered his father and married his mother – but the phrases on the right, with their pronouns and verbs, constitute little stories. In contrast to the inert statements on the left, they are enlivened by the narrative element of characters (*you* and *we*) taking actions.

Here are some practical applications of the story-telling principle. The next time you find yourself beginning a letter with the sentence, "Receipt of your letter of January 31, 1992, is acknowledged," try revising it to read, "I received your letter of January 31, 1992," or even, "Thank you for your letter of January 31, 1992."

Remember: Use character and action.

Here's another example: "There are some safety concerns about the purchased product and therefore, as a precautionary matter, a recall is in order." Not trace of human life to be found.

Now try sprinkling in a little character and action, and you get something like this: "Because we are concerned about your safety, we are taking the precaution to recall the product you purchased from us." Much improved, wouldn't you say?

Now, here's your assignment for the week: Find at least five sentences devoid of character, action, and human interest in your reading and writing, and revise them into sentences that tell a story. Don't forget to use character and action.

Good luck.

Mix it around to keep from being bland, boring

One of the most common goals I hear from people in my workshops is that they want to learn to express their thoughts with more emphasis. They don't want to write in a style that is bland and boring.

There are countless techniques for achieving this. Here are a few.

First, keep in mind the natural emphasis of the simple, declarative sentence (that is, a sentence with one main clause). The principle here is that the shorter the sentence, the greater its emphasis.

The same concept of brevity relating to emphasis applies to paragraphs, with a little twist: the shorter the paragraph, the greater the emphasis and the faster the pace. (Also, the more white space, the more inviting the page is to the reader). This is why, despite what you may have learned in school, it is perfectly acceptable to write a one-sentence paragraph – as long as you are doing it for stylistic effect.

But don't overdo it.

After all, a one-sentence paragraph by its very nature precludes full development of an idea, so it's best not to have too many of them. Furthermore, a series of one-sentence paragraphs, like a series of short declarative sentences, runs the risk of creating a choppy, staccato rhythm.

A second technique for vigorous writing is to use parallel structure to lend emphasis to your sentences. (Remember Ben's aphorism, "Early to bed. . ."?) This principle is particularly important when listing items under a colon, a popular format among business writers. Compare these two lists:

We have three goals:
1. Install a credit scoring system.
2. The loan committee should approve all dealers.
3. On-time distribution of the monthly management report.

We have three goals:

1. Install a credit scoring system.
2. Require loan committee approval of all dealers.
3. Distribute the monthly management report on time.

Notice the greater emphasis and momentum of the second list, which is presented in parallel format. Note too that the sentence is broken so that each item under the colon begins with a verb. This creates a sense of movement and energy, making the list a dynamic sequence of actions rather than a static series of nouns or conditions. It's a handy technique for adding some vim and vigor to your lists.

Another method to make your writing lively and interesting is to offer your reader variety. Simple, declarative sentences are an excellent tool for writing with emphasis, but a steady diet of simple, declarative sentences can be too much of a good thing. Likewise, a string of long, complicated sentences can be daunting to your reader. So vary your sentence length. A very short, four or five-word sentence in the midst of a string of longer sentences can lend special emphasis to your point.

The reader is stimulated by variety in other things as well, such as sentence length, sentence structure, paragraph length, and word choice. To illustrate this point, note how flat this sentence sounds: "He has the ability to learn these skills quickly and has shown interest in learning them."

The problem here is that the reader expected something new, something exciting at the end of the sentence, but the author instead served up a minor variation of a phrase just offered ("ability to learn . . . interest in learning"). Notice how eliminating this quick repetition picks up and enlivens the sentence: "He has both the interest and the ability to learn these skills quickly."

The rule is simple: the more variety, the more energy.

In other words, if you want to write vigorously and colorfully, mix it around a little. Don't bore the reader with a bland diet. Sameness can be stultifying.

Writing As Process

How to make writer's block less of an obstacle

I've been sitting here for two hours trying to write this column. And what do I have to show for my time? Not a thing. Nothing but frustration.

I keep going back and forth from my writing pad to my word-processing screen, hoping that changing the medium will somehow make the words flow. I've gathered and sharpened all the pencils I could find in the house. Nothing helps. I've even gotten down on all fours to work on a new trick I'm teaching my Old English Sheepdog, Molly. (I'm showing her how to push a toy baby stroller across the floor with her nose.) Any diversion at all seems to hold my attention better than my writing assignment.

In a word, I'm blocked.

I call a friend, who tells me my problem is obvious: confusion over my purpose in writing, insecurity regarding my audience, inadequate knowledge of my material, failure to approach writing as a process, and perfectionism coupled with negative thinking.

The solution, she assures me, is equally obvious. Here's her advice – not that it will do me any good.

Think of writing as a process. Writing is not a single-step event but a process with at least four distinct phases. These include pre-writing, generating text, revising text, and presenting text. You're more likely to get stuck if you try to write final copy in a single step, without, for example, first doing your pre-writing work: determining your purpose, understanding your audience, and knowing your material. Skip the first stage and you may find that the words just won't come. When this happens, the real problem, according to my friend, is not language but approach.

Allow yourself the freedom of an imperfect first draft. Hemingway (never one to follow his own advice) was fond of saying, "The only thing that matters about your first draft is that you finish it." In other words, just do it. Give yourself the benefit of sketching out a draft that is nothing more than a beginning. This frees you from the tyranny of perfectionism. It's a wonderful freedom. Once you've created a text, you can always go back and rewrite and polish and fuss over it. The idea is to "get it written, not right."

Develop good writing habits. My friend also told me that writing comes more easily if you write at the same time every day. Some of her friends even make appointments with themselves to protect their writing time. They believe that keeping a regular writing schedule helps their minds and bodies develop a kind of rhythm, so that when that time comes to write they are more likely to have the energy and concentration that writing demands. Some even reserve a certain place in their home or office where they do nothing but write. They don't balance their checkbooks there, and they don't talk on the phone there. When they sit in that certain place, it's time to write.

Think positively – about yourself and about your ability to write. The novelist Gail Godwin once told my friend about a trick she uses to silence that inner critical voice that we all hear sometimes. Godwin thinks of this self-censoring tendency in terms of Freud's notion of the Watcher at the Gate, a little creature that sits perched on the edge of your subconscious mind. Even as your thoughts are first taking shape, this creature says things like, "Stupid. Unoriginal. Doesn't sound right. Don't let it out." When Godwin hears this inner voice, she looks the Watcher at the Gate right in the eye and says, "Be quiet. I know you're there. You have a legitimate role to play, but you're too early. First I create. Then I revise."

Well, that's what my friend told me about overcoming writer's block. I hope you find her advice helpful. I don't. I don't think I'll ever get this column written either. Even if I do, it probably won't be any good.

"Bulldozing" leaves no time to be critical of writing

Well, I'm stuck again. I can't even think of a title for this. I was considering something like, "How to write a memo that's good enough without taking all damn morning to get the job done," but I decided that was dumb. Besides, I don't think newspapers should print words like *damn.* [They didn't.]

I've tried everything. I've switched from my pencil stub to my special Waterman fountain pen, from my blue screen with white characters to my green screen with yellow characters. Nothing seems to help.

So I call my friend, the one who always files her income tax return by January 15. When I explain my problem, she asks me if I'm a bricklayer or a bulldozer.

I tell her I don't understand the question.

"You've never heard the analogy?" She seems surprised. "Well, there are essentially two kinds of writers," she explains, "bricklayers and bulldozers.

"Bricklayers are writers who are incapable of going on to the second paragraph until they are completely satisfied with the first. They find it impossible to write Sentence 2 until Sentence 1 is absolutely perfect. For them, writing tends to be tedious, exhausting, and time-consuming.

"Bulldozers, on the other hand, charge right through the first draft. They just keep plowing ahead until they get to the end. They don't care what their text sounds like along the way because they know that once they've got the words down they can go back and revise. For them, writing is easy, enjoyable, and rewarding.

"So, which kind are you?"

"Me? Well . . . ah . . . more the bulldozer type," I say, stretching things a bit. "Except for today. Today I just can't seem to get started."

"No problem," she says. "You got five minutes? Good. I want you to write down a phrase and then keep writing without stopping for five minutes. Just write whatever comes into your head. Relax. Don't work hard. Just write. Don't worry about what it sounds like. Don't worry about spelling, punctuation, or grammar. Don't worry about anything at all. There are only three rules: You can't stop writing, you can't go back and read what you've written, and you can't change anything. Ready? Now write this down and keep writing until I call you back: 'The main purpose of this column is . . .'"

Well, what's five minutes? I ask myself. So I go ahead and try it.

When the phone rings, I have a sore wrist. But I also have two pages of scribbling and some new ideas for my article. More important, I'm now in the mood to write.

"Hey, that was great!" I say. "Where did you learn that trick?"

"It's nothing new," she explains. "In the 1930s Dorothea Brande called it effortless writing; in the 1970s Peter Elbow called it free writing; in the 1980s Natalie Goldberg called it writing down the bones. Personally, I like to think of it as spontaneous writing because that reminds me of the spontaneous imagination of the English Romantic poets."

"Interesting. But why does it work?"

"Well, Virginia Woolf used to say that writing at a gallop left her internal critics behind. What she meant was when you write without stopping there's no time to be critical. Even Yogi Berra knew the secret."

"Really? What did he write?"

"No, I mean when he played baseball. The next time you get stuck, just think of what he said about stepping up to the plate: You can't hit and think at the same time. Same goes for writing your first draft. See ya later."

I want to ask her some more questions, but she hangs up, saying she wants to put the finishing touches on her annual report before lunch so she can whip off a couple grant proposals before 5 o'clock.

After spontaneous start, you need an outline

The other day I returned to my office and found a message on my answering machine. The caller hadn't given his name, but the voice was familiar.

"I understand there's been quite a bit of talk down there in the Cities about free writing or spontaneous writing – or whatever you want to call it – you know, the Peter Elbow method where instead of making an outline you just start writing to see where your thoughts will take you. I hear you think it's a cure for writer's block."

Then I realized who it was: a writing friend who lives in the woods up North.

"Well, I guess that's a pretty good way to get started, but I want to tell you about another approach," his voice continued. "Up here in Bemidji, we call it the Norwegian School of Writing. Ever hear of it?"

There was a pause. I thought I heard a snicker.

"Like the farmers, we believe you've got to fence the field before you plow it. Same goes for writing. You don't just wander off in any direction. You need a plan – especially for business writing. Just wanted to give you the contrary point of view. Bye."

I was baffled. Ever since another friend had explained the technique of picking a topic and writing about it for five minutes without stopping to edit, I had been free writing every day – in fact several times every day. Well, to tell you the truth, my writing desk was covered with tablets of scribbled text and pages of printouts. And despite all the scribbling and typing, my report still wasn't getting written. All I had were tablets and pages of great ideas.

So I called my other friend, the one who had suggested free writing to me in the first place. I explained my predicament.

"Now that you've done your free writing, you need to make an outline," she said.

"I do?"

"Of course. Especially for business writing. How else can you begin to organize your material?"

It was the second time I had heard this advice in one day, so it must be true. I asked her if she had any tips on how to make an outline.

"It depends on what kind of outline you want. There are three main forms: scratch, topic, and sentence. But first you might want to try some listing, clustering, mind-mapping, cubing, dialoguing, or maybe even treeing. Or if you really liked the free writing exercise, I can teach you a variation called looping. It's up to you."

"Well . . . maybe I should just go ahead with the outline."

"Fine. Which variety?"

"Could I just have the plain kind?"

"Of course. Here's how you do it. Make a list of your main points. Then use your list to organize your material. Don't be afraid to modify your outline as you write. And don't feel compelled to include every bit of your material if you discover that something really doesn't fit."

"That's it?"

"Not quite. List the reasons you think your main points are important. Also, be sure to include relevant details and illustrations to support your arguments. Show the reader the same information that made you come to *your* conclusions – the more specific and concrete the better. This is especially important in persuasive writing, such as proposals and recommendations."

"Anything else?"

"Just one thing. Don't try to write perfect copy in your first draft. Just plow through until you get to the end. Remember: First you plant the seeds; then you cultivate the crop."

"Like the Norwegian farmers up north?"

"What?"

"Never mind. Now, what about all these sheets of paper?"

I tried to swallow back my exasperation. "I can't even see my desk. I can't even see the floor. I can't even find my dog."

"Oh, those. You can toss them. Or, better yet, use the reverse sides and do some more free writing!"

Ben Franklin and Malcolm X have something for you

What do Ben Franklin and Malcolm X have in common? Give up?

Both were language nuts. I know, you were probably thinking of more obvious similarities, but what you may not have realized is that both men devoted themselves to mastering the English language with a zeal that – well, it makes you wonder.

Take Benjamin, for example. It's one thing to decide you're going to teach yourself to write, but quite another to go about it the way he did.

One day when he was about 15, he relates in his autobiography, "I met with an odd volume of the *Spectator,*" a London journal famous for its lively wit and satire. He had never seen one before. He was so taken with it, particularly with the essays of Addison and Steele, that he determined to use it as a model:

"I took some of the papers, and making short hints of the sentiment in looking at the book, tried to complete the papers again by expressing each hinted sentiment at length and as fully as it had been expressed before, in any suitable words that should occur to me. Then I compared my *Spectator* with the original, discovered some of my faults, and corrected them."

That's not all. When he found he "wanted a stock of words or a readiness in recollecting and using them," he set a new challenge for himself:

"I took some of the tales in the *Spectator* and turned them into verse, and after a time, when I had pretty well forgotten the prose, turned them back again. I also sometimes jumbled my collections of hints into confusion and after some weeks endeavoured to reduce them in the best order before I began to form the full sentences and complete the paper. This was to teach me method in the arrangement of the thoughts."

In other words, by playing around with the writing of the pros he not only expanded his vocabulary but learned the fundamentals of organization and coherence. Was that guy crazy or what?

And then there was Malcolm. While doing time for burglary in the Norfolk Prison Colony, where he rediscovered both religion and books, he tells us, "I became increasingly frustrated at not being able to express what I wanted to convey in letters that I wrote, especially those to Mr. Elijah Muhammad." His solution: "I saw that the best thing I could do was get hold of a dictionary – to study, to learn some words."

Because he didn't know *which* words he needed to learn, he just started with the letter A and began copying "everything printed on that first page, down to the punctuation marks." He was so pleased to encounter words that he "never knew were in the world" that he went on and copied the next page. Eventually, he copied the entire dictionary, from A to Z.

I know what you're thinking. Who was nuttier: Benjamin or Malcolm? And what did they accomplish with this fanatical commitment to language, anyway?

Not much, really. Ben, who described his facility in writing as "a principal means of my advancement" and referred to his printing press as "the foundation of my fortune," changed the course of history by persuading the French to support the Colonies during the Revolutionary War. Malcolm took the natural linguistic ability that had made him "the most articulate hustler out there" and developed it into a mastery of language that made him one of the most dynamic, inspirational orators of twentieth-century America.

Now, assuming that you've misplaced your copy of the *Spectator* and that you don't have time to copy the dictionary, here's how you can apply Ben and Malcolm's lesson.

The next time you read a memo that knocks your socks off, that is written with the kind of precision and clarity that you've always wanted to achieve in your own writing, don't just dump it in the recycling bin. Put it in your good writing file. And then go back from time to time and see if you can determine what it was that made it work so well. You might even want to copy it over, word for word.

Who knows what might happen?

Writing in Delicate Situations

To write or not to write: A question of good management

It has often been said that good managers are good communicators. And good communicators, one might add, are people who know when to write and when not to write.

One of the greatest problems with business writing – aside from imprecise and wordy language, meaningless jargon, faulty sentence structure, weak paragraphing, buried purpose statements, poor organization, and distracting errors in punctuation, spelling, and grammar – is that there is simply too much of it. Most of us in the business world feel oppressed, if not overwhelmed, by the daily blizzard of routine correspondence, reports, and miscellaneous documents that threatens to bury us in an avalanche of unnecessary or long-winded communications.

I once heard a speaker at a management conference remark, "The best advice I can give you about good business writing is this: Whenever possible, don't do it."

Now it may seem curious for someone who makes his living as a writing consultant to say this, but I happen to agree. Too often we put things in writing when we would be better off saying them in person. Before committing our thoughts to the written word, we need to ask a fundamental question: Should we write at all?

In *Writing for Results,* David Ewing offers some helpful guidelines for making this decision. Certain situations and certain types of communication, he points out, are better handled orally, either by phone or in person. The time to write, Ewing suggests, is only when seven criteria are met:

1. You have a clear and practical purpose in mind
2. Writing is the most efficient method of accomplishing your objective
3. Y*ou* are the right person to write
4. The *time* is right
5. You've taken into account the *riskiness* of the written word

6.   You've taken into account the *rigidity* of the written form

7.   You've taken into account the *insufficiency* of the written word, given its one-way dimension

The problem with written communication, Ewing explains, is that it may be too rigid: "On many occasions it is important that you be able to 'feel your way' with your audience. You can do this if you are talking, but not if you are writing."

It isn't hard to imagine situations in which this is true. Resolving complex budget issues, where information may be confusing or incomplete, is an example of where the ready give-and-take of spoken communication is useful. (Of course, once things are sorted out, there's no better method of recording your decisions and agreements than the written word.) Problems involving people with sharply differing perspectives and approaches might likewise be resolved more readily if the parties would talk to each other without first locking themselves in by declaring their positions in writing.

Not only is the written word more rigid than the spoken word, but it is also riskier. "Unlike words spoken in conversation," Ewing observes, "the written word stays indelibly clear for an indefinite period. If it is photocopied for hundreds of other people to read in addition to the target audience, it still loses none of its authenticity, as the spoken word does when repeated from person to person."

The result, according to Ewing, is that in writing you "assume a greater risk of permanency than the speaker does – you have to live much longer with your words. You would be a fool not to appraise this risk seriously on those many occasions when relationships are delicate, sensitive, or charged in some other way that may lead you to regret your words as soon as someone has read them."

To put it simply, it is often better to talk than to write. In *The Effective Administrator,* Donald Walker suggests that, when problems get complicated, instead of sitting down at your typewriter or word processor, "get everyone concerned in the same room." And just talk.

How to make enemies and start wars with your writing

The first rule about writing in anger is: Don't do it.

Nine out of ten times it will get you into trouble. Words that might seem perfectly reasonable and justified in the heat of passion often sound excessive and unprofessional in the cold light of day.

For the sake of argument, however, let's assume that this time (just this once!) your best option is to write. You've weighed the risks, you've made certain you have your facts straight, and you've decided that this is one of those rare occasions when the best course of action is to express your anger in writing. Here's how to do it.

1. Question your own motives. Are you genuinely trying to find a solution, or is your real purpose to make the other person as angry as you are? If the latter is your goal and you are successful, all you have is two angry people.

2. Use language that conveys your anger and explains your position but that doesn't insult or attack your audience. Remember: Your purpose is to resolve the issue, not to seek revenge.

3. Don't use the shotgun approach. Focus on the issue at hand. Forget about past wrongs and what may seem like a host of related issues. Stick to the point.

4. Express your unhappiness in terms of actions taken and their consequences, rather than in terms of behaviors or personal shortcomings. It's much easier for people to admit that they made a mistake than to acknowledge that they have a character flaw.

5. Avoid escalating the conflict. One of the most common ways of raising the stakes is to send a copy of an angry letter to someone's boss or colleagues. Once you go public with your anger, however, it may take a formal truce to end the conflict.

Now, all this advice is based on the assumption that your goal is to state your case as forcefully and firmly as possible, to clear the air, and to get on with things. But if what you're really after is revenge, then I would suggest a somewhat different approach:

1. Never question your own motives or try to see the world from your adversary's perspective. Why confuse yourself with self-doubt? Such soul-searching is a sign of weakness. Instead, focus your attention unflinchingly on the righteousness of your own position and the machinations of your evil adversary.

2. Go for the jugular. There are three sure-fire ways to make people furious: Insult their intelligence, attack their competence, or question their integrity. So don't fool around. Hit all three buttons in a single letter and you'll have them clenching their fists and gnashing their teeth.

3. Use extreme language that puts your opponent on the defensive. Ultimatums are especially effective here. "If you ever do this again, I'll . . ." is a phrase that can't be beat for turning up the heat. There's really no way you can complete it without backing both yourself and your opponent into a corner. "Why-didn't-you?" questions are another great way to make your adversary feel so defensive that counterattack seems the only sensible option.

4. After you have written your angry letter, send it without delay. Your prose never sounds as polished and devastating when you read it after you've cooled off, so get it out while it's hot.

5. Let the whole world know how angry you are. The more people you can get to take sides, the longer you can prolong the conflict. The principle here is to make your displeasure known to the largest number of people in the shortest time possible. This foreshortens that awkward period in which something might actually get settled.

Follow this advice carefully, and I guarantee you'll make your opponent as angry as you are. Who knows? If you work hard at it, you might even make an enemy for life.

Writing to threaten and intimidate will cost you

We pay a tremendous price, both financial and personal, for negative and threatening communications. Think of the time that is wasted every day in this country, the untold energy that is squandered in countless businesses, industries, and government agencies, by people behaving defensively because they feel threatened or under attack.

What is the cost of defensive behavior?

One answer is provided by Jack Gibb, who back in 1961 started a kind of revolution in communications theory and organizational development with an article entitled "Defensive Communication," published in *The Journal of Communication.*

In that watershed article, Gibb pointed out that individuals who feel threatened or insecure in a group give some attention to the common task, but they also devote an appreciable portion of their energy to defending themselves: "Defense arousal prevents the listener from concentrating upon the message. Not only do defensive communicators send off multiple value, motive, and affect cues, but also defensive recipients distort what they receive."

Gibb discovered that "As people become more and more defensive, they become less and less able to perceive accurately the motives, the values, and the emotions of the sender." The result: a measurable decline in the accuracy of the message, both as it is sent and as it is received, as well as a downward spiral in interpersonal relations.

"When insecure," Gibb explained, "group members are particularly likely to place blame, to see others as fitting into categories of good or bad, to make moral judgments of their colleagues, and to question the value, motive, and affect loadings of the speech which they hear." In other words, when people are made to feel defensive, they tend to interpret all information in a negative light. And as we all know, negative energy begets negative energy.

In contrast, behavior that appears to be spontaneous and free of deception is "defense reductive": "If communicators are seen as having a clean id, as having uncomplicated motivations, as being straightforward and honest, and as behaving spontaneously in response to the situation, they are likely to arouse minimal defense.

"The more 'supportive' or defense reductive the climate," Gibb continued, "the less the receivers read into the communication distorted loadings which arise from projections of their own anxieties, motives, and concerns. As defenses are reduced, the receivers become better able to concentrate upon the structure, the content, and the cognitive meanings of the message."

Here's how you can use Gibb's findings to check your own style of writing and communication – as well as that of your associates – to see if it is "defense arousing" or "defense reductive."

Consider a written passage (or a recent conversation) and ask yourself which of Gibb's six paired attributes below best describes the language employed. Does the language convey:

evaluation	or	description
control	or	problem-solving orientation
strategy	or	spontaneity
neutrality	or	empathy
superiority	or	equality
certainty	or	provisionalism?

If the tone of the language is best described by the attributes on the left, the communication is more likely to arouse defensiveness and to undermine trust. If it is best described by the attributes on the right, it is more likely to reduce defensiveness and to inspire trust.

Let's take some examples.

Consider these two statements: "The only way to increase productivity is for you to get your people to work harder." / "Do you and your staff members have any thoughts about how we can increase productivity?" Which statement conveys control and which takes a problem-solving approach?

Here are two more: "Your report is due in my office by noon today." / "I need your report by noon so I can include it in our presentation tomorrow morning." Which conveys superiority and which conveys equality?

Can you find examples of your own? Chances are, whenever you read something that makes you feel uncomfortable or insecure, the language, according to Gibb's definition, is "defense arousing."

Even "business writing" can deal with feelings

One year ago today the *Star Tribune* printed the text of Brian Coyle's letter to his colleagues on the Minneapolis city council revealing that he was HIV positive. The first paragraph of his letter read:

"For most people, acquired immune deficiency syndrome (AIDS) is something very far away, but for me it has been a daily reality for nearly a decade, and I have decided to come out publicly as an HIV (Human Immunodeficiency Virus) infected person in order to educate people and to improve my chances for survival."

In his second paragraph he explained that he wanted his friends to be "the first to know" that the May edition of *Minnesota Monthly* magazine (to appear the next day) would carry a cover story disclosing his illness, and that Channel 5's KSTP Investigative Team would simultaneously begin airing a series about his struggle.

I remember how impressed I was when I read that letter, how touched I was by Mr. Coyle's courage and grace, how moved I was by his sensitivity and eloquence. He succeeded, as few do, in finding just the right words to convey not only the facts of his situation but also the complex and conflicting feelings – from his "conscious decision to nurture wellness" to his desire "to focus on the deeper value of life" – that human beings experience when confronted with the inevitability of death.

In the year since Mr. Coyle's letter appeared, I've often thought about how it might serve as a model of good writing, but I have struggled over how to present my thoughts without showing disrespect for the author or trivializing his tragic death. And yet his letter *is* a model of good writing. It was no doubt written with a great deal of thought and care.

With all due respect to the author, then, I would like to venture a few remarks about why I consider his letter such an effective communication.

First, it was timely. In fact, timeliness was the whole point. Mr. Coyle wrote to forewarn his associates and friends that he was suffering from a fatal illness before the story was released to the public. His letter was an act of thoughtfulness and consideration – admirable traits in any circumstances but noble when exhibited by the dying. By taking the initiative to communicate in writing to those closest to him, he was able to control the timing, the medium, the tone, the style, and the emphasis – to communicate his message exactly the way he wanted to.

Second, his language was natural and direct, even conversational. The voice we heard was not that of the faceless bureaucrat nor that of the slick politician. It was a genuine, human voice that used honest, direct statements such as "In retrospect, I guess I suspected something was happening to my body as early as 1981 or 1982" and "AIDS forces you to investigate what you really want your life to be." It was the voice of a successful public figure and community leader who was not afraid to speak from the heart.

Third, his letter did more than impart information. It offered a sense of values and purpose. It went beneath the surface and got to the essence of things. As is characteristic of our most inspiring leaders, his letter revealed a broader vision – in this case, Mr. Coyle's goal of leading a life based on determined optimism, commitment to community service, and lasting friendship.

Finally, his letter was considerate. Rather than lead off abruptly with his news, which he knew would shock and upset his reader, he began with a general statement, a bit of courteous indirection – "For most people, acquired immune deficiency syndrome (AIDS) is something very far away" – which gave the reader a moment to focus and prepare for the next telling phrase – "but for me it has been a daily reality for nearly a decade."

It is true that business writing should be clear, concise, and to the point. We have been taught to write pragmatically, to lead off with our purpose statements, to get to the point. But it is equally true that the very best writing, even "business writing" addressed to professional associates, takes into account the feelings of both the author and the reader.

Venting your anger and psyching out your enemy

Remember last Friday? It was one of those gorgeous, October days that we live for in Minnesota, the kind of day that makes your heart ache to be outdoors savoring those last fleeting hours of a passing season.

Temperatures were pushing into the 80s. You were hoping for an early departure from the office. You couldn't wait to get out on the golf course or take a stroll around the lake or maybe just get home and put your feet up where you could soak up the sun and breathe in the fresh air. Ah, life seemed so beautiful.

And then you got that memo. Blind-sided, once again, by that jerk down the hall.

Why do these things always happen on Friday afternoon? (They don't, actually. The other time they happen is the day before a long-awaited vacation.)

I remember the time one of my associates wrote a letter to my boss complaining about something one of my staff members had done. He described the offending action as an example of "the bravado of bureaucrats run amok," a phrase that rankles me to this day (though, I must admit, it has a catchy cadence). He copied the letter not only to me but also to my boss's boss, to the head of another office within our division, and to the head of an office outside our division. All this without a prior word to me.

Here's what you should do (and what I should have done) the next time someone does something to you that really gets your goat.

Don't leave the office until you've dealt with the issue (*and* with your anger). Sit down at your computer and bang out a memo to your tormentor *before* you leave for home. Don't wait to cool off, don't tell yourself that you'll deal with the problem on Monday, and – whatever you do – don't try to be professional. Just ask yourself: How am I feeling?

You're furious; that's how you're feeling! Now, get that anger into your writing.

In your memo, say everything and anything you've always wanted to say to that big-mouthed, arrogant, chicken-hearted bozo who has ticked you off. Don't hold anything back. If you're having trouble getting started, try something like this: "If you had a brain, you'd take it out and play with it!" Or maybe this: "If you knew what made this company work, you wouldn't be here!"

Get the idea? Go ahead, stretch yourself a little. Anything goes! Be completely unprofessional, intemperate, and uninhibited.

Feels good, doesn't it? OK, now you've had your say. Put the problem out of your mind. Relax, go home, and enjoy that marvelous weekend.

And, of course, don't send the memo.

That's step 1. Step 2 requires more discipline and restraint. It's also a lot less fun, but I have it on good authority that it works.

Part 2 is a "little laboratory experiment" recommended by the psychotherapist Carl Rogers. Writing in the *Harvard Business Review* in 1952, Rogers described an extraordinarily simple technique for taking the tension out of conflicts:

"Each person can speak up for himself only AFTER he has first restated the ideas and feelings of the previous speaker accurately and to that speaker's satisfaction."

In other words, before presenting your own point of view, you must "achieve the other speaker's frame of reference – to understand his thoughts and feelings so well that you could summarize them to him."

Sounds simple, doesn't it? "But if you try it," Rogers said, "you will discover that it is one of the most difficult things you have ever tried to do."

The payoff, however, may well be worth the effort: "Once you have been able to see the other's point of view . . . you will find the emotion going out of the discussion, the differences being reduced, and those differences which remain being of a rational and understandable sort."

Why not give it a try? Even if it doesn't work, just think how it will help you psych out your enemy.

How to say no without turning friends into enemies

Wouldn't it be nice if we could always say yes?

"Yes, of course you can have that bonus" (even though I've already promised it to your associate, who works much harder than you do).

"Yes, of course you can purchase that new color copy machine" (even though it costs $8,000, we don't need it, and our supply budget is already $5,000 in the red).

"Yes, of course you can take a week off to attend that conference in Hawaii" (even though this will be your third out-of-town conference in the past three months).

No one likes to be told no. And – as most managers and supervisors can attest – no one likes having to tell people no either.

But when that fateful time arrives (as it does for every good person in authority), when you have no choice but to turn someone down, to break someone's heart, to risk making an enemy for life – here are some tips (based on more experience than I care to remember) that might make it easier for you to say that dreaded word: No.

■**Before saying no, be sure that you haven't made up your mind prematurely.** No one likes working for a boss whose first response is always no. Don't be afraid to take some time to make your decision. If you are unsure, disclose your misgivings, request more information, or ask to hear the arguments again.

■**Show respect for the person making the request.** If the request is appropriate and the person has the right to make it, acknowledge that right. Try to distinguish between the person making the request and the request itself. If you like the person, make that apparent. Look for ways to be reassuring even as you say no.

■**Consider saying no in person rather than in writing.** Taking the time to walk down to someone's office is a way of conveying your respect. Furthermore, a face-to-face conversation will allow you to react to facial expression and body language and perhaps to soften the blow.

■**If you find it difficult to say no, admit it.** Statements such as "I hate telling you no" or "I wish I could say yes," if perceived as genuine, can be disarming to the person whose request you are denying.

■**Be clear and unambiguous.** If you mislead someone into thinking that you are going to say yes, you only increase that person's disappointment.

■**Be firm and decisive.** Don't change your mind just to please someone when you know the answer should be no. Have the courage to stand by your convictions.

■**State your reasons for denying the request, but don't over-elaborate.** A simple, respectful no is usually easier to take than one justified by a lengthy explanation. Also, the more you talk, the more likely it is that you'll say the wrong thing, especially if you're feeling awkward about having to say no.

■**Stick to the issue.** Have you ever noticed that when you deliver bad news, people tend to find fault with the way you handled the request, to criticize you for other decisions, or to remind you of past disappointments? It's human nature for people to complain when they're unhappy. Your best response in these situations is to avoid (for now) broad discussions of right and wrong, your style of management, the quality of your working relationship, etc.

■**Expect disappointment and even anger on occasion.** People may respond angrily or inappropriately – no matter how carefully and skillfully you present your message. They may criticize the *way* you told them, but the real issue is often *what* you told them. Perhaps the only consolation in cases like these is to remind yourself that you cannot control the outcome of every encounter.

Remember: Your job is to make the best decisions you can and to communicate those decisions as clearly and respectfully as possible.

How to write a bad-news letter without being brutal

What's wrong with this letter?

"Dear John: You're fired. Please clear out of your office by 3:00 p.m. today. Thank you for 15 years of truly outstanding service. I appreciate your commitment and hard work. Good luck in finding employment elsewhere during these tough economic times."

Whatever else you might say about the letter, it meets the standard criteria of good business writing: It is clear, concise, and free of distracting errors in punctuation or grammar. The purpose statement is unambiguously presented in the opening sentence. The language is polite – even friendly, in a perverse sort of way.

The letter's flaw (a grievous one) is that it is brutally direct. Most managers wouldn't consider writing such a letter without taking into account the reader's feelings. They would use a little tact or indirection. They would provide a buffer.

A more respectful and humane approach might be: "Dear John: Despite your 15 years of truly outstanding service, you're fired. Please clear out of your office by 3:00 p.m. today, etc."

Well, maybe more of a buffer than that is needed, but you get the idea.

The next time you have the unpleasant task of writing a bad-news letter, remember this: Your challenge is to deliver the bad news in a way that maintains your reader's goodwill.

As Schell and Stratton point out in *Writing on the job*: "You may be turning down what seems to be a poorly conceived and hastily written proposal, but five years from now the person who submitted it may have an idea that will make your company rich. You want that person to think well of you and your organization even though you turned down the proposal."

Here are some guidelines that will help you achieve that delicate balance between clarity and consideration:

■**Take particular care with your tone.** The *way* you say

something is sometimes as important as *what* you say. You don't want to be so brief that you sound curt or brusque, nor so lengthy that you sound overly solicitous.

■**Be firm and unambiguous, but not blunt or brutally direct.** Don't bury or disguise bad news to the point that your reader is left wondering about your meaning, and don't deliver it in a way that leaves your reader reeling from shock. Be clear but tactful.

■**Avoid lengthy explanations, excuses, and apologies.** As a rule, less is better. Your reader deserves an explanation, but if you go on too long you risk raising issues that could be used against you.

■**When possible, offer assistance, suggestions, or support.** As Rosalie Maggio suggests in *How to say it,* you might offer to help at a later date, suggest someone else who might be able to provide the same assistance, or find some other means to lessen your reader's disappointment.

Beyond these *dos* and *don'ts,* here's how to organize your letter according to a four-part formula:

■**Buffer or introduction.** Lead off with a statement that prepares your reader for the bad news. In my example above, you might open with a reference to the poor business climate or mention other measures you have taken to cut costs. If you are writing a refusal, you might begin by thanking your reader for making the request.

■**Bad news.** Be unequivocal but kind. Use wording such as *I regret, unfortunately,* or *disappointing.*

■**Explanation or follow-up.** Present the reasons for your decision briefly. If appropriate, offer suggestions or assistance.

■**Goodwill closing.** Offer your best wishes. End on a positive, encouraging note. "Good luck in finding employment elsewhere during these tough economic times," for example, could be rephrased to read, "Despite these tough economic times, I'm sure that someone of your experience and talent will succeed in finding a satisfying position."

In short, the secret to writing a bad-news letter is taking into account your reader's feelings. Ask yourself: How would *you* like the news to be presented to *you*?

Writing Collaboratively

How to be a good critic to those who write for you

Critics have been putting down writers – sometimes with great wit and scathing cruelty – for as long as writers have been writing.

Two hundred years ago Samuel Johnson (who wrote one the first dictionaries of the English language) offered this devastatingly clever appraisal to a would-be author: "Your manuscript is both good and original; but the part that is good is not original, and the part that is original is not good."

Even Groucho Marx got into the act when he stung S. J. Perelman with this unforgettable zinger: "From the moment I picked your book up until I laid it down I was convulsed with laughter. Someday I intend reading it."

Few people can match the wit of a Samuel Johnson or a Groucho Marx. But if your goal is to help people write successfully on the job rather than put them down or make points at their expense, you don't have to be witty. All you have to do is follow these six principles of constructive criticism.

1. Purpose. Remember your purpose: to help the people who write for you produce the best document they are capable of producing, not to establish your superiority as the better writer or to demand that the author write exactly as you do. Good critics tend to think of themselves as coaches rather than judges.

2. Tone. Good critics take care to use a positive tone. They don't just mark the errors or problems they see (for example, "awkward" or "poorly worded"). Instead, they offer suggestions for correcting them (for example, "Try this wording: . . ." or "Offer more explanation here."). Consider your own experience: Do you find it easier to write for a sympathetic or a hostile reader? For which reader are you more likely to do your best writing?

3. Emphasis. Good critics tend to be more descriptive than evaluative or judgmental. They approach errors as problems to be solved rather than as points to be tallied in their assessment of the writer's worth. An example of descriptive comment is: "Your meaning here isn't clear to me. Explain or illustrate your point." An example of evaluative comment is: "This is irrelevant and confusing."

4. Scope. Good critics address the author's purpose as well as make text-editing suggestions. They try to go beyond the surface problems of a text (punctuation, grammar, and word choice) to deeper issues of purpose, approach, logic, and organization. Recognizing that editing text is easier than producing it (just as reviewing books is easier than writing them), good critics try to help the author not only with the easier but with the more difficult parts of the writing process.

5. Balance. Writers need both specific suggestions and general comment. Good critics try to strike a balance: They offer specific recommendations for altering the text as well as more general explanations of what aspects of the writing worked and didn't work for them.

6. Clarity in expectations. When making assignments, good critics are clear and explicit about their expectations. It's more efficient – and easier on the author's ego – if you communicate what you want *before* rather than *after* the author has written and submitted an assignment. Two good ways to communicate your expectations are to offer examples of the kind of writing you want and to provide not only oral but written guidelines. In other words, if you want clear writing, give clear instructions.

From my own experience, both as a teacher who has worked with more than 2,000 business professionals and as a writer who has collected more than his fair share of rejection slips, I would say that the real mark of a good editor is someone who can offer a close, critical reading of a text while leaving the writer's dignity intact.

Giving writing assignments without bruising egos

How many times have you found yourself in this situation?

You give a writing assignment to a staff member. You explain what you want and when you want it. Your employee seems to understand the assignment. But when the deadline rolls around, you're shocked by what is given to you.

You ask yourself: Why can't the people who write for me do a better job? Why can't they get it right the first time? *What's wrong with them?*

Well, it could be a number of things. It could be that they need help in developing their writing skills. Maybe they need more time to complete their assignments. Maybe they just don't appreciate the importance of good writing.

On the other hand, maybe the problem is *you*.

It could be that *you* are not doing everything *you* could be doing to help your staff members write to the best of their abilities. In writing, as in every other area of staff performance, you have an important role to play in ensuring your employees' effectiveness.

Here are some guidelines that will help you be more successful in giving writing assignments – so that your employees can be more successful in giving you what you want.

■Describe the purpose of the assignment clearly. What is obvious to you may not be obvious to your staff members, especially if they have not been involved with the project from the beginning.

■Explain why the assignment is important. Whenever possible, link its relevance to a broader purpose, goal, or mission. In writing, as in all facets of your business, employees want to be reminded that their contributions are vital.

■If you want something written a certain way, make that clear from the beginning. Why play a guessing game? It's easier on your writers' egos – and on your patience – if you make your expectations explicit.

■Explain in detail any special instructions. Offer illustrations and examples if needed.

■If there are important points that need to be emphasized, make these explicit. You might even want to provide an outline of major points to be covered.

■If you know something about the audience that might influence the writer's approach or tone, share that knowledge.

■Indicate what length you have in mind. No one enjoys drafting a five-page document only to be told that the document can be no longer than one page.

■Depending on the assignment's complexity, give your instructions both orally and in writing.

■Invite questions and comments.

■Specify a deadline. If the project is urgent, explain why and, again, link it to a broader purpose.

■For a more involved project, request that a rough draft be submitted at some point prior to the deadline, so that you can offer comments and help shape the project as it develops.

■Whenever possible, avoid rewriting text extensively (unless you are looking for a permanent job as copy editor). Instead, ask your writers to revise according to your comments and instructions, so that they can learn to produce better copy in the future.

■Emphasize the importance of clear, concise writing that is professional in appearance and free of distracting errors in grammar and punctuation. If your writers tend to keep making the same errors (such as lack of subject-verb agreement or incorrect possessive forms such as *it's* for *its*), make a list of these errors and explain how to correct them.

■Finally, be positive and encouraging. If you feel confident of your employees' abilities to do a good job writing, be sure to convey that confidence. Even when working with your weaker writers, a positive approach will generally get better results than a negative one.

Following these guidelines will not guarantee that your staff members will produce quality writing. But it will stack the odds in their favor – and in yours.

How to promote good writing in the workplace

One of my more interesting assignments as a writing consultant was the time I worked with managers at First Bank, St. Paul, to help them develop strategies for promoting good writing among their item-processing staff.

I had already offered several workshops for this division when I got a call from Kevin Shaw. He said he wanted me to do another workshop, but this time he had an idea for a little different approach.

"We were thinking," he explained, "that now that you've worked directly with our staff members, it might make sense to have you train our managers to do the teaching. That way, they could reinforce the writing principles and practices that you've already introduced. What do you think?"

Teach the managers how to teach writing? Hmmm. It made good sense to me. In fact, once Kevin suggested the idea, it seemed so obvious that I wondered why no one had asked me to do it before.

So we got to work. Here's how the workshop went.

We started with the basics. First we reviewed some principles of composition. Then we discussed how to identify and correct the most common errors in business writing (lack of clarity, missing or buried purpose statements, wordiness, misplaced commas and apostrophes, nonparallel structure in sentences, and lack of agreement between subjects and verbs and between pronouns and antecedents).

Next we explored ways of writing in stages (techniques such as pre-writing warm-ups to generate ideas, writing straight through a first draft without stopping to revise, and standard highlighting techniques for making the text more inviting to the reader, as well as some tricks of the trade for revising and proofreading).

Finally, we got to the heart of the matter: What can managers do to promote successful writing on the part of their staff members? Our list of recommendations went something like this:

■**Emphasize the importance of good writing.** Creating an environment in which good writing is encouraged and valued, we concluded, is critical. One means of accomplishing this is simply to discuss writing concerns and issues with your staff. Show an active interest. Let it be known that good writing counts, that you consider it a reflection of your company's commitment to quality.

■**Lead by example.** Demonstrate competence in your own writing. As one manager put it, "There's no getting around it: If I expect my staff to produce quality writing, I need to be more conscientious in my own efforts."

■**Provide models of good writing.** In addition to serving as a role model, you can assist your employees by providing examples of what you consider good writing. You can even develop standard formats for reports, executive summaries, etc., so that your staff members "don't have to reinvent the wheel" with every assignment.

■**Offer constructive criticism.** You will get better results from your writers if you think of yourself as a coach rather than a judge. One means of providing this support is to edit your staff members' writing projects yourself. Another way is to encourage your staff members to exchange writing samples and edit each other's work on a regular basis.

■**Approach writing as a process.** Once you understand that writing is best approached as a process involving several distinct stages, you can use that understanding to your advantage. For one thing, you can invest more time and effort at the *front* end of the process by communicating your expectations. For another, you can request that your staff members submit drafts to you several days before the deadlines, to give you an opportunity to review the work in progress and to allow your writers time to make final revisions. As one manager put it, "If you want quality, don't expect immediate turnaround."

This brief summary of our deliberations should be enough to get you started. So put on your teacher's hat and start teaching!

Writing
Inclusively

Use precise language that is fair to both sexes

What would you do if a colleague sent you the following note?

"Be prepared for a stormy meeting. Susan is furious with McDowell. Although a pleasant and charming colleague, she impresses me as a woman with a quick temper and a sharp tongue."

A. Talk with your colleague before the meeting to get more details.

B. Talk with Susan to find out what is troubling her.

C. Talk with McDowell to see how he is feeling.

D. Arrange for your secretary to summon you from the meeting to take an "urgent" call.

E. Send your colleague a copy of Casey Miller and Kate Swift's *Handbook of Nonsexist Writing.*

Depending on the situation, any or all of the first four choices might be the reasonable and prudent thing to do. But in any circumstances the correct answer is E. Your colleague (whether male or female) could no doubt benefit from the handbook, which not only presents compelling arguments for using inclusive language as a matter of fairness and precision, but also provides practical suggestions and helpful alternatives on how to accomplish this.

As Miller and Swift point out, "Only recently have we become aware that conventional English usage, including the generic use of masculine-gender words [such as 'chairman'], often obscures the actions, the contributions, and sometimes the very presence of women. Turning our backs on that insight is an option, of course, but it is an option like teaching children the world is flat."

So, what's wrong with the language in the note? Plenty.

First of all, it violates the fundamental rule of nonsexist usage: equal treatment of both sexes. It makes nonparallel references to *Susan,* a woman, and to *McDowell,* a man, rather than parallel references to both, as in "Susan is furious with

George" or in "Smith is furious with McDowell." Depending on the context, either first or last names may be used, but not first names for women and last names for men.

Second, the phrase, "Susan is a woman who," calls attention to gender, although gender has nothing to do with the point being made. Miller and Swift call this problem a "superfluous sex qualifier," and they compare it to "gratuitous modifiers" such as *male nurse* and *lady attorney,* which offend because they imply that certain professions are appropriate only to one sex.

In an example cited by Miller and Swift, the *Oswego Palladium-Times* misplaced a modifier in the sentence, "Meals are prepared under supervision of a dietician packaged in disposable Styrofoam containers." When *The New Yorker* chided, "Never mind her predicament. Are the meals any good?" it scored a point but fumbled the ball by inadvertently implying that all dieticians are female.

Finally, the language in the note is sexist in yet another way. It depicts Susan (or Smith) as a quick-tempered or highly emotional person. (The word that comes to mind here is "spitfire.") Would we describe a man with the same language? Almost certainly not. In choosing words to describe the actions of women and men, we should beware of a cultural tendency to describe women in conflict as "quarrelsome" or "peevish" but to depict men in similar situations as "angry" or "willing to stand on principle."

The rule of thumb here is straightforward and easy to apply: Unless there is a legitimate sex-linked difference, use the same language that you would use in reference to the opposite sex. A good way to check your text, and to guard against unconscious bias, is to write a draft in which you switch the sex of the person being described. Try it the next time you write a performance appraisal or a letter of recommendation; then examine your language. Would you describe a male colleague as "pleasant and charming" but possessed of "a quick temper and a sharp tongue"?

In other words, are you using language that affords equal dignity, status, and recognition to both sexes?

How to avoid the "generic he" but not be awkward

If you or your employees are writing sentences such as "We are committed to serving the customer and meeting his needs," you're probably losing customers. And if you or your associates are writing sentences such as "If anyone in your office has any suggestions, tell him to see me," you're probably creating ill will among your employees.

As most of us are well aware, using masculine pronouns *(he, him,* and *his)* to refer to both sexes is no longer considered acceptable English usage. We recognize that the "generic he" (increasingly called the "pseudo-generic he") does not in fact evoke both sexes in the minds of many readers and listeners. Its use leads not only to ambiguity and misinterpretation but to outright exclusion of females.

Consider, for example, a job notice that reads: "The successful applicant will be able to express his ideas clearly and persuasively." What message is sent to the prospective applicant who is female? How is she to know whether the employer intends *his* to mean *his or hers,* or whether the employer is suggesting that only male applicants need apply? In the same way, what message is sent with statements such as "A successful C.E.O. knows how to inspire his workers," or "Every manager should know his own strengths and weaknesses"?

Since the publication of Casey Miller and Kate Swift's *Handbook of Nonsexist Writing* in 1980, public attention has shifted away from debating whether or not change is needed to discussing which alternatives represent the best, most natural and least intrusive means of writing inclusively.

We have found that new constructions such as *s/he* or paired pronouns such as *he or she* may eliminate ambiguity, but they also can be awkward and distracting, especially when repeated several times in the same sentence or paragraph. Some writers have sought to overcome this awkwardness by simply alternating masculine and feminine pronouns (one time using *he,* the next time using *she*).

Joseph Williams does this throughout his book, *Style: Ten Lessons in Clarity & Grace.* And when he explains why sentences with short subjects and long predicates work better than sentences with long subjects and short predicates, he uses the feminine pronoun to good effect: "If we create a long subject, our reader has to hold her breath until she gets to the verb."

A skillful writer or speaker can pull this off. But too often these well-intentioned attempts to use inclusive language distract the reader or listener from the primary message. The reader or listener may even find herself watching the writer or listening to the speaker to see if he will remember to switch genders – more like keeping score at a baseball game than attending to what is being communicated.

Here, then, are a few helpful suggestions for writing inclusively without writing awkwardly.

Use plural pronouns. "A good manager listens to his staff members." / "Good managers listen to their staff members."

Replace the masculine pronoun with an article *(a, an, or the).* "The customer has a right to his opinion." / "The customer has a right to an opinion."

Use the second person. "If a person works hard, he might succeed." / "If you work hard, you might succeed."

Eliminate the masculine pronoun. "When the consumer buys our product, he deserves good service." / "The consumer who buys our product deserves good service."

These alterations in wording may seem cumbersome at first, but with practice they come easily and naturally. If on occasion you find yourself wondering if it is worth all the effort, remember that in taking care to use inclusive language your goal is no different from your purpose in writing generally: to convey your message in clear, precise, unambiguous language that neither confuses nor offends the reader.

Having fun with *The Dictionary of Bias-Free Usage*

OK, let's get picky. No, more than that – let's get picky, petty, and downright persnickety.

I'm referring to Twin Cities author Rosalie Maggio's *The Dictionary of Bias-Free Usage: A Guide to Nondiscriminatory Language.* Her purpose in compiling this dictionary, which she claims contains 5,000 entries and 15,000 alternatives, "is not to tell anyone how they must speak or write" but to put "all the biased terms in the language in one place for handy reference" and to help us all do a better job of recognizing and avoiding biased language.

Can you believe it?

Well, hold on to your hats (I mean bonnets) – I happen to think Maggio's critique of the English language is brilliant – and her dictionary marvelous.

In fact, every time I pick up her book and browse through it, I find myself – well, fascinated. Entertained. Edified. I begin with the intent of just having a quick look and end up totally engrossed.

Here's a sampling. In place of *businessman,* Maggio suggests *executive, business executive/associate/profession-al/leader,* or the plural, *people in business, businesspeople.* In place of *career girl/career woman,* Maggio recommends *professional, careerist,* and others. Her comment: "When tempted to use 'career woman,' consider how 'career man' would sound and then handle the situation the way you would have for a man." Likewise, she recommends that *spry* be avoided as a word "reserved for older people to indicate that they are livelier than you would expect at their age."

Maggio condemns *mannish* and *he-man* (the latter "perpetuates stereotypes and expectations of men that are often false and damaging") for the same reasons she rejects *womanish* ("a vague and pejorative stereotype"). In their place, she recommends the obvious: Use adjectives that convey your precise meaning, words such as *blunt, abrupt, direct, aggressive, hardy, rugged, muscular, domineering,* or *fussy, choosy, fastidious, anxious.*

She exonerates certain expressions that are suspect – *stand pat:* "nonsexist; 'pat' is not a person"; *charley horse:* "retain; this popular and instantly grasped term is harmless as sex-linked terms go"; and *smart aleck:* "although this expression comes from the man's name Alexander and seems to be used more often of men than women, it is acceptable for both sexes." But she declares others guilty by association – *niggardly:* "although by definition and derivation . . . completely unrelated" to the racial slur, the term is nonetheless "too close for comfort to a word with profoundly negative associations."

In response to countless expressions such as *David and Goliath, Davy Jone's locker, Tom Thumb, Jack Frost, Hobson's choice, Walter Mitty, Mickey Finn, Mickey Mouse, Sneaky Pete, Midas Touch, wise as Solomon, and poor as Job,* she offers the same advice: "When using expressions like this, be aware of how many are male-based. Some of the time use female-based expressions, creative expressions of your own, or alternatives."

Maggio recognizes that breaking old habits can be difficult, even frustrating, and that taking things to an absurd extreme can be ridiculous ("He/she ain't heavy, Father/Sister; he/she's my brother/sister"). But she also argues that it can be very satisfying: "One of the most rewarding – and, for many people, the most unexpected – side effects of breaking away from traditional, biased language is a dramatic improvement in writing style. By replacing fuzzy, overgeneralized, cliché-ridden words with explicit, active words. . . you can express yourself more dynamically, convincingly, and memorably."

Well, that sounds pretty good to me. And now, I have a challenge for you. I want you to think big.

If each of you commits yourself to using inclusive, bias-free language in your business writing, it could transform American commerce – no, more than that, it could revolutionize the whole of American society and culture. Ten years from now I want to hear people everywhere marveling at the impeccable precision and the indisputable impartiality of your language, and wondering in amazement where and how

the revolution got started.
Don't disappoint me now!

Priorities: Good grammar or bias-free language?

In a recent column on how to avoid sexist language, I quoted Rosalie Maggio, author of *The Dictionary of Bias-Free Usage* as saying that her aim in writing the book was to put "all the biased terms in the language in one place for handy reference," not "to tell anyone how they must speak or write."

One of my more observant readers, Noel R. White (a teacher in Stillwater) noticed that Maggio had used the plural pronoun *they* in reference to the singular antecedent *anyone*.

Well, as we all know, a pronoun (a word that takes the place of a noun, such as *he, she,* or *they*) must agree in person and number with its antecedent (the word to which the pronoun refers – in this case *anyone*). In other words, using a plural pronoun with a singular antecedent is considered bad grammar.

As Ms. White pointed out, Maggio could have avoided the problem by revising "to tell anyone how they must speak or write" to read "to tell anyone how to speak or write" or "to tell people how they must speak or write."

Furthermore, she wrote: "I expected your column . . . to make the point that bias-free language is *not* achieved simply by using grammatically incorrect constructions to avoid the he/she dilemma."

She went on to ask, "Has it become acceptable in business writing to use expressions that are technically incorrect to avoid bias in language? . . . You're the expert – what do you say?"

Well, it's hard to ignore such a straightforward question (especially if you want to keep passing yourself off as an expert). The issue of pronoun/antecedent agreement is a hot topic among linguists, composition teachers, and other guardians of the language.

The problem is, of course, that modern English lacks a genderless third person personal pronoun. The first person (*I, me* in the singular, *we, us* in the plural), the second person (*you,* both singular and plural), and the third person plural *(they, them)* can all be used to refer to males and to females. But the third person singular pronoun *(he, she, him, her, it)* simply doesn't give us what we need: a personal pronoun that we can use to refer to both sexes. Thus, the debate.

To work around this deficiency, we have essentially three options. One, we can continue to use the "generic he" to refer to both sexes (but then we risk confusing or offending our audience). Two, we can perform linguistic gymnastics to avoid the masculine pronoun (that is, use *he or she* or *s/he,* change both the pronoun and its antecedent to the third person plural, use the second person in place of the third person, etc.). Or three, we can declare it grammatically acceptable to use the third person plural pronoun in place of the singular pronoun when we want to refer to both genders (for example, *to each their own* rather than *to each his own*). Maggio takes the third option.

Well, the time has come for me to enter the fray. Here's my position (but I want you to know that I plan to take another crack at this topic in my next column).

In your attempts to work around the masculine pronoun when referring to both genders, you are better off to respect pronoun-antecedent agreement, especially in more formal types of business writing. In speech or informal writing, you are granted more leeway with the rules. In those situations, you may, depending on your audience, decide that it is permissible to venture the singular *they.* But for most types of business writing, I recommend that you play it safe.

Remember: Your goal as a business writer is to get your message across without distracting or offending your reader. The fact is, Ms. White is not alone. Many of your readers expect not only inclusive language but grammatically correct constructions.

Every writer wishes they could solve this issue

In my previous column I responded to a reader who faulted Rosalie Maggio, author of *The Dictionary of Bias-Free Usage*, for using *they* in place of a singular pronoun, as in "The aim of this book is not to tell anyone how they must speak or write."

As I pointed out, the problem is that modern English lacks a genderless third person personal pronoun. The first person (*I, me* in the singular, *we, us* in the plural), the second person (*you*, both singular and plural), and the third person plural *(they, them)* can all be used to refer to both sexes, but the third person singular pronoun *(he, she, him, her)* cannot.

The advice I offered was this: In your attempts to avoid the masculine pronoun ("to tell anyone how *he* must speak or write"), you are generally better off not combining the plural pronoun *they* with singular antecedents such as *anyone*. At least for now. Certain rules, however, are changing, and this particular issue is one on which many linguists, writers, and teachers disagree.

As Maggio points out, the National Council of Teachers of English (NCTE) has given its blessing to the singular *they* in certain circumstances: "In all but strictly formal usage, plural pronouns have become acceptable substitutes for the masculine singular."

Another expert, Albert Joseph, however, considers the NCTE's position scandalous. In "Guidelines for nonsexist writing" (issued by the International Writing Institute Inc. of Cleveland), he laments: "Incredibly, the NCTE recommends 'Every secretary must be aware of *their* responsibilities.'"

According to Joseph, this is not only "terrible grammar" but also "unnecessary." Worse yet, "Once poor grammar is endorsed for special situations, where does it stop? Who decides if a situation is special enough? This academic permissiveness is an invitation to the 'anything goes' attitude in language usage."

Well, in my view Joseph (whose notion of English grammar is more traditionalist than mine) is being alarmist. I applaud those who would urge us to be on guard against sloppy and careless usage, but I don't believe that using the singular *they* as a matter of principle will lead inevitably to the "decline and fall" of the English language.

Besides, if you think about it, the singular *they* is not really all that outlandish. We do, after all, have a precedent in English. Having dropped the second person singular *thou* from modern usage, we now use *you* for both singular and plural meanings, and we seem not particularly troubled by the potential for ambiguity (except perhaps in the South, where *y'all* clearly signifies plural).

Moreover, as Maggio and others (including Casey Miller and Kate Swift in *The Handbook of Nonsexist Writing*) point out, there is historical precedence for the singular *they*. In fact, it wasn't until the nineteenth century that a consensus developed against its use. Until then, many writers (including Shakespeare) commonly used *they* for both plural and singular pronouns.

Finally, that so many speakers and writers are using the singular *they* suggests a need for it. Our language is missing a crucial element, a genderless third person singular pronoun, and our everyday usage reflects our instinctive desire to fill that gap. More and more people are simply finding the singular *they* the easiest, most natural substitute for our missing pronoun.

Often, the most radical changes in a language are the ones that evolve the most gradually. Many of us are already saying, "anyone . . . they," (I sometimes use this combination in speech, depending on the occasion and the audience), and I suspect that in another five or ten years many more of us will be writing it, even in the most formal usage.

Not until our better writers like Maggio start using the singular *they* as a matter of principle, however, will people see it as conscious, intended usage rather than as carelessness or bad grammar. Only then will it become fully acceptable – and only then, I suspect, will we have a truly workable solution to the *he/she* dilemma.

Writing for Results

How to word salutation when recipient is unknown

In response to my columns on the importance of using inclusive, nonbiased language, Richard H. Swiler of Hayward, Wisconsin, wrote:

"Quite often I find it necessary to correspond with businesses, government bureaus, and other entities whose gender is unknown. When I was in high school it was taught that 'Dear Sir' was proper and acceptable, but I am sure that there is a more genderless salutation in use today.

"To me the use of 'Dear Sir/Madam' seems stilted and 'To Whom It May Concern' one step away from putting a note in a bottle. Tell me, please, what is the accepted, generic salutation in correspondence to an unknown entity?"

Well, that's a good question, one I'm often asked. Here's my advice.

First, as you suspected, *Dear Sir* and *Dear Gentlemen* have gone the way of the wooly mammoth, and *Dear Sir/Madam* and *Dear Gentlemen/Ladies* may be inclusive but they sound old-fashioned.

Your best alternative by far is to find out the person's name. This isn't always possible or practical, but it's often worth the effort. Whether a query or a complaint, your letter generally will get more attention and will be taken more seriously if it is directed to a particular person. Whenever possible, then, get the person's name, even if it means making a phone call for the information.

Once I have the person's name, you might ask, how do I handle the title – *Mr., Ms., Mrs.?*

If the person has a professional title (*Dr., Professor, President,* etc.) and you know it, use that and the last name, followed by a colon. (A comma should be used after the salutation only in less formal writing.) If you don't know the person's professional title, the preferred usage is to address a man as *Mr.* and a woman as *Ms.,* regardless of marital status. As pointed out in *The Business Writer's Handbook* (Third

Edition, 1987), "If a woman has expressed a preference for *Miss* or *Mrs.,* however, you should honor her preference."

If, on the other hand, you can't tell from the name whether the recipient is a man or a woman (as in *Chris* or *Kim*), you may combine the professional title with the last name, as in *Vice President Nichols* or *Administrative Assistant Carter,* or simply omit the title and use both the first and the last name, as in *Dear Chris Carlson* or *Dear Kim Bell.*

What about those times when it is impractical to get the person's name or when I am writing a letter addressed to multiple recipients?

You have a number of options here. First, you may use an appropriate professional title after *Dear,* such as *Human Resources Manager, Customer, Director, Subscriber, Home-owner,* etc. In some cases, *Dear Friend* or *Dear Colleague* may be suitable. A third option is to use the memo format *(TO: Chief Marketing Representative),* or simply to omit the salutation entirely.

Finally, you might just decide that your best alternative is the one that is "only one step away from putting a note in a bottle": *To whom it may concern.* It may not be personal, but it's inclusive and it gets the job done.

The secret ingredients of a customer relations letter

Here's the situation.

Your company promised to deliver 22,000 Good Writing software packages (whose components include a grammar checker, readability assessor, style replicator, fact checker, unabridged dictionary, intelligent template, and grant-proposal compositor with a guaranteed 20% success rate) to a customer by January 15, in time for a post-holiday national promotion, but that date has come and gone and you still have not delivered your product. Then this morning your chief programmer informed you that a deadly virus has infected your system and production will be delayed at least another two months. You have just gotten off the phone with your customer, whose reaction to the news was neither gracious nor dignified, and now you must write a follow-up letter trying to cast things in the best light possible.

Where do you begin?

Well, the good news is that you don't have to begin at the beginning. As unlikely as it may seem to you during these times of crisis, you're not the first person who has had to write a letter to an angry customer. Other people before you have faced the same unpleasant assignment, and you can learn from their experience.

Most successful customer relations letters are written according to a standard 5-part formula. (Although my version of the formula differs somewhat from Sherry Sweetnam's, I first became aware of it from her advice on how to write letters of apology in *The Executive Memo: A Guide to Persuasive Business Communications*.) Those components are:

Goodwill Greeting and Reference. Open your letter on a positive note and in a personal tone. Be specific in your references to the problem and to any previous communication. If you are responding to a complaint, make it clear that you understand the problem and, if appropriate, apologize (both here and below).

Here's an example: "I appreciated the opportunity of talking with you this morning about delivery of your Good Writing programs. I understand your frustration over the delay and I apologize for the inconvenience."

2. Statement of Empathy or Apology. Use language that acknowledges the reader's perspective ("I'm sure you felt . . . ," "I understand that . . ."). Be careful not to unintentionally imply that the customer is at fault. At the same time take care not to overstate your culpability. The idea is to be forthcoming and gracious while guarding yourself against legal action.

If you *are* placing the blame on the customer (which you should do only in rare circumstances and only for very good reasons), be diplomatic. Remember, a single negative word carries as much weight as ten positive ones.

3. Explanation of the Problem's Cause. Keep this part brief. Remember that *you* are the expert and that the customer expects *you* to solve the problem. Overly elaborate, detailed explanations tend to sound like excuses.

4. Good News/Bad News and Documentation. Be clear and specific about what action you have taken or will be taking to correct the problem. When offering good news, you can abbreviate the empathy statement, as described above. When offering bad news – information that you suspect will anger, disappoint, or fail to satisfy the customer – explain briefly what prevents you from resolving the issue.

5. Goodwill Closing & Reassurance. In your closing, remind the reader of your respect and goodwill, and stress the importance of your continuing relationship. Because the reader expects this customary tag at the end, omitting it may cause the reader to doubt your commitment and sincerity, no matter how polite and respectful you have been in the rest of your letter.

Here's an example: "Again, thank you for letting us know of your concern. We appreciate your business and want to provide you with the best service possible."

There you have it – but don't forget the heart of the enterprise. The real secret to writing a good customer relations letter is to write from your reader's perspective. The rest is easy.

In customer relations letters, put the reader first

Have you ever heard the expression, "Give a three-year-old a hammer, and all the world needs hammering"?

Well, I have a corollary: "Give a businessperson a fax machine, and all the world needs faxing."

Know what I mean?

Here's a variation on the same theme: "Give a company a computer, and every part of its operation requires a weekly report."

If you have ever been afflicted with the task of producing (or receiving) these infinitely dispensable reports, you know how anesthetizing they can be.

Several years ago I had an exchange with a life insurance company that had a serious case of computer-generated-report syndrome. Twice each month, with each contribution from my paycheck, I was sent a statement of my account. But with my retirement more than 25 years away, it seemed outrageously wasteful to produce and mail all those reports, particularly for a plan that offered only limited investment options.

Finally, in exasperation, I wrote and begged for deliverance. Instead of generating 600 reports over 25 years, I pleaded, why didn't they report quarterly, or at most monthly, and credit the savings to my account?

I mailed the letter with little hope that my protest would be taken seriously or that the company would offer a satisfactory response. To my surprise, I received a letter that was completely disarming.

Not only was it written according to the standard 5-part formula for a customer relations letter (goodwill greeting, empathy statement or apology, explanation of the problem, good or bad news statement, and goodwill closing), but it did a superb job of acknowledging my point of view. It put me, the reader, first. Both in language and tone, it demonstrated that the writer could see the situation as I saw it, that the writer recognized the validity of my perspective.

In short, the letter succeeded because it was written from the "you viewpoint."

It began this way: "Thank you for your letter of February 22, 1988. We appreciate your input and suggestions."

Nothing fancy about it as openings go, but it did the job. It gave me the impression that someone was listening. It did what every good customer relations letter should do. It conveyed the simple message: "I hear you."

Because my complaint had been acknowledged, I felt open to what the writer had to say. In contrast, imagine how I might have felt if the letter had begun: "I have here before me your letter of February 22, 1988. The reason we cannot comply with your request is . . ."

Perhaps worse than feeling disappointed that no remedy was available, I would have felt snubbed by the writer's failure to acknowledge or validate my point of view.

Other statements in the letter reinforced the "you viewpoint": "We have received feedback like yours from several other participants" and "Everyone's opinion certainly has merit." The letter's "goodwill closing" was written in the same empathetic and validating tone: "Again, thank you for your feedback. We will keep you informed as any enhancements are made to the reporting of your account."

As Richard Weaver points out in *Understanding Business Communication,* to assume the reader's viewpoint, "writers must both think and write in terms of the reader."

"Using this principle involves much more than simply using the words 'you' and 'your' in your letters – although these pronouns help. The best way to achieve a 'you viewpoint' is to stress the reader throughout your letter."

The letter I received did this so skillfully that I hardly noticed one detail: The only good news offered was the assurance that "We are exploring the possibility of modifying our system." It wasn't much, but I didn't really care. By then, I was won over by the letter's tone and wording.

Oh, by the way, in case you're wondering: Within a year or two the company did convert to a quarterly accounting system. But by then I had forgotten I had ever been unhappy.

A simple recipe for terrific instant thank-you letters

What could be easier than writing a thank-you letter? All you have to do is say, "Thank you," and sound as though you mean it. What could be simpler?

But if thank-you letters are so easy to write, why are they often written so poorly? And why does it seem to take forever to write a good one?

Here's the problem: There are only so many ways to say "thank you." This makes these seemingly straightforward letters surprisingly difficult to write. Although your message is simple, you don't want to sound ungrateful or terse by writing a letter that is too short. On the other hand, you don't want to risk sounding insincere or glib by padding your letter with clichés or hollow-sounding language.

In short, you face a dilemma.

Writing thank-you letters may seem like a chore, but they are vitally important to the operation of your business. Thank-you letters can go beyond their primary purpose of creating good will. As Schell and Stratton point out in *Writing on the Job: A Handbook for Business & Government,* they can be used as follow-up letters "thanking a potential customer for visiting your showroom or for the telephone inquiry, or thanking a new customer for an order, telling when the merchandise can be expected – and of course reminding the reader of your presence."

So, to make your life a little easier, the person you're thanking a little happier, and your business a little more profitable, here's a four-step recipe you can use to whip off terrific-sounding thank-you letters in five minutes flat.

Thanks the First Time. Simply tell your reader that you appreciate his or her contribution. Fresh, original language is always preferable to clichés, but there's nothing wrong with beginning, "Thank you for . . ." or "I am writing to express my sincere appreciation for . . ." etc. "On behalf of . . ." is another standard opening that works well because it underscores your role as representative of a group or organization.

Specific, Personal Reference. Refer specifically to what the reader has done for you. Emphasize the particular benefits derived from his or her contribution. Include at least one personal detail that recognizes the contributor as an individual.

General Reference. Remind your reader of your broader mission or goal. Point out the importance of his or her contribution in this broader context.

Thanks Again, and Goodwill Message. Again express your appreciation for your reader's contribution and stress the importance of your continued relationship. This is your opportunity to reiterate: "I value you as a person, I appreciate your gifts and talents, and I place great importance on our relationship."

Sound good? Let's give it a try. Here's the body of a thank-you letter that lacks spice:

"Thank you very much for your presentation on fund-raising. The audience really liked it and found it very useful. Thanks again for taking the time to meet with us."

Pretty bland, wouldn't you say? Not a smidgen of that certain je ne sais quoi that we all crave.

Now, put that uninspired version in the pot, add the four ingredients mentioned above, mix thoroughly, simmer on low heat for 5 minutes (30 seconds in a pressure cooker or microwave), and here's what you get:

"On behalf of the National Society of Fund-raisers, I am writing to thank you for your excellent presentation. It was truly inspiring. One person remarked, 'That was the most useful presentation I've ever heard!' Several others commented that they appreciated your positive approach and enjoyed your lively sense of humor. Your recommendation to open an appeal letter with an attention-getting device like a Johnson Box is something we can use to help increase our revenues in the coming year. Again, thank you for taking the time to share your wonderful insights and experience with us."

Just add paragraph breaks to taste and *voila:* a thank-you letter with a little pizzazz!

How to write a fund-raising letter that will never fail

Here's how to write a fund-raising letter that is guaranteed to bring in the bucks. Just follow these simple steps.

■**Catch the reader's attention within the first three to four seconds.** Lead off with your strongest material. Use action words and powerful messages that have a sense of urgency and encourage action on the part of the reader. Remember: "Feelings first; facts follow."

■**Consider using a Johnson Box.** Named after the New York copywriter, a Johnson Box is a concise, provocative summary presented as an attention-getting block of text before the salutation. Its main purpose is to get your prospect to read your letter.

■**Personalize your letter.** According to Roland Kuniholm in *Maximum Gifts by Return Mail,* "Good personalization is copy that sounds personal, not just a few words the computer picks out of its file and drops into a line of text. It must sound like you really know the donor as a person."

Although your letter "may go to 100,000 donors," Kuniholm reminds us, "it is read only by one at a time. The closer you can make your letter sound like a true, one-on-one communication, the closer you are to the ideal of personalization – with or without computer fill-ins."

In *How To Write Powerful Fund-Raising Letters,* Herschell Gordon Lewis puts it this way: "The strongest word in fund-raising is *you.*"

■**Engage the reader by calling for an immediate response.** Arrange your copy so that it leads the reader through the message to take the action you want. Make it convenient for your donor to give. Include a return address envelope and indicate a suggested amount or a range of donations.

■**Consider using a promotional or involvement technique.** Kuniholm explains: "The idea is to involve the prospect in some activity other than making a gift – for example, sending their senator a postcard, or filling out a survey form. The theory is that the 'involvement' activity will be easier to convince the prospect to do than making a gift. But, once 'involved,' the prospect will be more apt to make a gift."

■**Don't be afraid to write a long letter.** Many professional fund-raisers have found that long copy "pulls" better than short copy. A long letter allows you to make your request more than once: in the Johnson Box, in the opening, one or more times in the middle, in the closing, and in the postscript or P.S. (which, in an appeal letter, gets high readership and therefore, according to Kuniholm, is used "not so much as an additional minor thought, but as a restatement of some strong selling point.") As many experts advise: "State your purpose early and often."

■**Be sure to emphasize the benefits of contributing** – both to the donor and to the receiving organization. Even when a gift is small, tell what it will accomplish. Also, remember that your letter is a natural opportunity to create a greater awareness of your organization or cause.

■**Finally, test the effectiveness of your appeal letter.** Try it out on a test group. At the least, show it to your associates and get their comments. You might even want to use the A/B mailing list approach to increase your chances for success. This involves sending your most successful previous letter and your new letter to every other person on your list. Then compare the results and continue using whichever letter was more successful.

■**And now for the guarantee.** Mail a letter to yourself. (Don't forget your zip code and a stamp.) When it arrives, open it, read it, and take out your checkbook. Ask yourself how much your campaign really means to you – give it some deep thought, listen to your heart – and write a check for whatever amount you would like to have as your guarantee.

Like I said, it never fails. And what could be simpler?

Grant proposals: Writing is just part of the process

The only thing you need to do to get a grant is write a good proposal. Right?

Wrong.

In fact, the word "writing" in the phrase "writing a grant proposal" is misleading. Words such as "planning," "orchestrating," and "implementing" more accurately describe what it takes to secure a grant.

Whether you are applying to the federal government, a private foundation, or a corporation, writing the proposal is only one step in a lengthy process. For convenience, let's divide the process into four stages.

■**Stage 1: Evaluating your idea and your ability to implement it.** The first thing you need to do is assess the value of your idea. Is it needed? Does it solve an important problem? Is it timely, unique, and innovative? Can you or your organization realistically follow through on what you are proposing?

As reported in the *Chronicle of Higher Education* (Jan. 14, 1987), foundations generally base their decision to finance a project on five criteria: the quality of the people involved, the significance of the problem, the importance of the solution to the problem or the idea being proposed, the stature of the sponsoring institution, and the reasonableness of the price.

How does your idea measure up to these criteria?

■**Stage 2: Finding a likely funding source.** Many grant proposals are denied simply because they are submitted to the wrong agency. Read carefully a prospective funder's guidelines, eligibility requirements, and evaluation criteria. Inquire by phone or brief letter to see if a granting agency has any interest in your project. Request a list of previously financed projects. You might even want to ask for guidance and advice on how to develop your proposal. (Many professional grant-proposal writers will tell you that involving the agency's staff at this stage can create interest in your project.)

■**Stage 3: Gathering internal and external support.** This is the stage in your planning when you get people involved, both inside and outside your organization. Make sure you have the personnel needed to carry out your project. Find out if they are committed to your idea. Depending on the nature of your project, you might want to assemble a board of advisers or solicit letters of support from well-known authorities.

■**Stage 4: Drafting, revising, and submitting your proposal.** Structure your proposal according to the guidelines provided by the granting agency. If no form or guidelines are provided, follow this standard 10-part format: title, summary or abstract, introduction, description of the problem, proposed solution and anticipated outcomes, methods or rationale, personnel and facilities, project evaluation, budget, and appendix.

Now (finally!) you're ready to begin writing. Here are some tips:

■Emphasize why you or your organization is the best qualified to solve the problem.

■Support your proposal with concrete and specific documentation, but don't overdo it.

■Present your strongest arguments and most compelling documentation first.

■Anticipate the reviewers' questions in articulating your rationale.

■Concentrate on what you think is the weakest part of your proposal. Often this is the budget.

■Be consistent in style and format throughout your proposal.

■Make sure your proposal is complete, free of errors, and attractively presented. Visual aids such as charts, graphs, and tables are generally appreciated by readers.

■Before submitting your proposal, ask colleagues and experienced grant-proposal writers to read and critique it.

Well, it's quite a process, isn't it? I don't mean to discourage you from giving it a try, but consider this: "Writing" the proposal is the easy part. If you get your grant, the hard work will have just begun.

Does anybody know why lawyers write the way they do?

Why do lawyers write the way they do?

I've been asked that question so many times that I decided to see if I could find out. Here's what I discovered.

At the University of Minnesota Law School bookstore I was astonished to find the same theme in every book I picked up: "Good legal writing is simply good writing."

In *The Little Book on Legal Writing,* Alan Dworsky advises, "Don't imitate casebook legalese when you write a memo or brief. Live lawyers don't write like dead judges." In *Plain English for Lawyers,* Richard Wydick argues that "Legal writing should not differ (without good reason) from ordinary, well-written English."

Furthermore, parts the table of contents in Shapo, Walter, and Fajans' *Writing and Analysis in the Law* looked as if they could have been lifted from any standard writing handbook: "Whenever Possible, Use Short, Concrete Subjects; Keep Your Sentences Relatively Short (under 25 words); Maintain Parallel Sentence Structure (Parallelism); Avoid Misplaced and Dangling Modifiers; Eliminate Unnecessary Words."

Eliminate unnecessary words? I looked again at the cover to make certain I was holding a book on legal writing. If this is how legal writing is being taught these days, I wondered, *why do lawyers write the way they do?*

I called one of my lawyer friends and asked, "What gives?"

"Well," she said, "law is like any other profession. Some people have had good training, and others haven't. Some write well, and others don't."

Not only did her explanation make perfect sense, but it was rendered, I noted, in short, easy-to-understand sentences that followed impeccable parallel structure. Needless to say, I was mightily impressed.

But still I doubted that I had uncovered the whole truth.

Then I read in Charrow and Erhardt's *Clear & Effective Legal Writing* that although some of the unique characteristics of legal writing "reflect the complexity of legal concepts and the nuances of the legal process," other characteristics survive only because of habit, including "overly long, complicated sentences, intrusive phrases and clauses, redundant phrases, poorly organized sentences and paragraphs, and a host of similar problems."

Charrow and Erhardt identified these causes:

■**Archaic constructions.** "Certain aspects of legal language," they noted, "have evolved separately from the rest of the English language." Other phrases and clauses, such as "malice aforethought" and "revoking all wills and codicils by me made," come from "grammatical constructions that are no longer in general use."

■**Precedent.** Legal language comprises certain "words, phrases, or larger structures whose meanings have been 'stabilized' through legal interpretation" and that "appear to embody the power of the law." Once the courts have interpreted these words and phrases in a particular way, lawyers tend to play it safe and keep using the same "frozen" language.

■**Coupling of French and Latin terms with English terms.** This peculiar type of redundancy evolved "as the use of French and Latin began to give way to English in the courts." Fearing that "some of the highly specialized meanings of the legal vocabulary would be lost," the lawyers of the time were reluctant to drop the French and Latin as they began using English.

■**Sociological factors.** The authors explained that "the ritualistic quality of some legal discourse" is intended to underscore the power of the law. "A society needs laws, and legal incantation may help persuade people to follow them."

Charrow and Erhardt's conclusion: "There may be legal reasons (either because of precedent or statute) for retaining many terms, but there are few valid legal reasons for clinging to Latinisms (prima facie, supra); strings of synonyms (null and void; any and all; rest, residue, and remainder); or archaic words and phrases (witnesseth, thereinabove, hereinbefore)."

With this, I knew, my search had ended.

So from this day henceforward I will acknowledge and confess, give, devise, remise, release, forever discharge, and bequeath the aforesaid knowledge for the rest, residue, and remainder of my days on this earth.

Res judicata et nolo contendere.

Writing for Effect

Metaphors are fine, but avoid clichés like the plague

The person who first looked out the window and exclaimed, "Look! It's raining cats and dogs!," introduced a wonderful figure of speech into the English language. Who would have thought to capture the essence of a downpour by comparing it to animals tumbling pell-mell from the sky?

It was a brilliant metaphor (a figure of speech containing an implied comparison) – when it was first used. But now, after billions of repetitions, the comparison has lost its luster. Over time it has become a dull, worn-out cliché.

("Cliché," by the way, comes from the French word for the "stereotype" plate used in printing. In reference to language, a "cliché" is a phrase or expression used so frequently that it has become trite and tedious.)

In business writing you face a predicament. How do you know when to use a metaphor to help you express your thought more vividly and memorably? And how can you tell when a once-original metaphor has crossed the line and become a tired and worn-out cliché?

It may help to consider some examples.

Here's a good metaphor: "The state is at a crossroads." That sentence was written by a budget analyst in the State Department of Finance. She used the image of "a crossroads" to emphasize the need to choose between a policy based on lower spending and one based on higher taxes.

Here's a bad metaphor: "We want to hire only the best applicants, so we are cherry picking the cream of the crop." That was written by a personnel manager of a trucking firm. He used the image of "cherry picking" to underscore his company's emphasis on quality.

Here's a terrible metaphor: "Given our employees' tendency to fly off the handle, we must nip their outbursts in the bud before they run rampant." That was written by the president of a Minneapolis consulting firm (me). I used it to illustrate how a truly rotten metaphor can be made even worse by mixing images – and as William Safire reminds us, "Take the bull by the hand, and don't mix metaphors."

I don't mean to ride a dead horse, but sometimes even seemingly good metaphors can backfire if they are used too frequently. George Ball, former chair of Prudential-Bache Securities Inc., was so famous (or infamous, depending on your perspective) for his colorful and quirky memos that they came to be called "Ballisms" or "Ballspeak." He once described his recently downsized company as a lean, light "cruiser" darting about among Wall Street's fat battleships. In subsequent memos he referred to this new profile as "Light Cruiserism."

Not everyone, however, appreciated the colorful comparison. As reported by *The Wall Street Journal,* some employees got "seasick": "One colleague returned a light-cruiser memo to Mr. Ball with the message, 'If I see the light cruiser-stormy seas analogy again, I think the whole crew will toss their cookies over the ship.'"

Why does one metaphor work and another fail? Why does one reinforce the author's message and another detract from it?

The answer, in my opinion, is simplicity. Some of the most famous metaphors in the English language are also the most natural. Consider, for example, Shakespeare's metaphor, "All the world's a stage," or these similes (metaphors that use "like" or "as"): "O my love's like a red, red rose" (Robert Burns), "My heart is like a singing bird" (Christina Rossetti), and "I wandered lonely as a cloud" (William Wordsworth).

Here's my advice for business writers: Use metaphors that reinforce or clarify your meaning without distracting your reader. Show restraint. Most often, the metaphors that flop are the ones that are overdone, contrived, or inappropriate for the subject or context. There is a critical difference between a metaphor that makes a gentle turn in the road and one that reaches out a giant hand and slaps you in the face. (Ouch!)

I ask you: Which of those last two metaphors worked for *you?*

Puzzling puns can make your reader go to pieces

I've been running with the same group of guys for almost ten years now. We start at the Minneapolis campus of the University of Minnesota and head south along the Mississippi River on what must be one of the prettiest urban running routes in the country.

The last time I ran with my fellow landscape panters, it was a cool day with a brisk north wind. After we crossed the Lake Street bridge and turned north we had the wind in our faces, but running south with the wind on our backs was a breeze.

"Now there's a good topic for your column," my friend Tom Swift said subjectively. Tom is a marvelous wordsmith, famous for his adverbial puns.

"Unintentional puns in business writing," he went on heedlessly. "Like the financial analyst who wrote to her client, 'I have a capital idea for increasing return on your investment.'"

"No, thanks. I wouldn't touch that apple for all the world," I said adamantly. "I have more serious topics to discuss in my column. Even curiosity will not tempt me."

"Oh, I think you should do it," Justin Case said uncharacteristically. Justin Case is an insurance broker who – as you may have guessed – doesn't believe in taking chances. "You could write about the homeowner who refused to use circuit breakers."

I thanked them for their suggestion and said I would think about it. Then our conversation turned to the presidential debates.

Reed Session is an economics professor who not only runs over the noon hour but rides his business cycle to and from campus. Although Reed hadn't mentioned it, I knew that he was planning to play golf this afternoon. I could tell by the fairway look in his eyes.

"Well, whatever the candidates say about our economy," said Reed sensibly, "it's obvious that unemployment is just not working."

Justin Case agreed.

"Take the farmers. Whenever the price of sugar goes up," Justin said in a candied tone, "they start raising cane."

"Precisely," said Reed pointedly. "The market was off twelve points yesterday."

"No, it was off two points short of a dozen," said Tom tensely.

"No it wasn't. When I get back to my office, I'll dig out my newspaper and prove it to you," Reed said gravely.

D. Artie Porker is an agricultural engineer who has little patience for politicians. He gave a snort.

"If Abraham Lincoln were alive today," he said mournfully, "he'd roll over in his grave."

"Our only hope is to elect Perot," said Tom hoarsely. "He's the kind of lone cowboy this country needs."

"I don't know," said D. Artie dumbly. "You can lead a horticulture, but you can't make him think."

By now I was getting winded.

"Where do you guys find the fortitude to run this fast?" I asked breathlessly.

"We usually find it somewhere between three-titude and five-titude," said Reed figuratively.

I felt like throttling him, but I'm no practical choker.

"How did you ever get tenure, anyway?" I demanded.

"It was easy," he replied. "It comes right after nineure."

"Eureka!" shouted Justin Case.

"You don't smell so good yourself," said Tom dryly.

By now I was wheezing and coughing.

"Come on, Steve. Keep going. It isn't the cough that carries you off. It's the coffin they carry you off in."

Well, that did it for me. Maybe I *will* try to write that column on unintentional puns in business writing, but I couldn't bake a bun if my wife depended on it, so I need your help.

Jest for the pun of it, I want you to send me your favorite examples of what the Greeks called paronomasia. Don't be ashamed. The more atrocious the better. As Samuel Johnson once wrote:

If I were ever punished
For every little pun I shed,
I'd hie me to a punny shed

And there I'd hang my punnish head.
If I'm not too punished by what you send, I'll share the worst/best groaners with you in a future column.

The power of positive thinking makes for good writing

We had spent a glorious fall day touring the meticulously restored buildings of Williamsburg, Virginia, listening to enthusiastic and knowledgeable guides explain in intimate detail how the people had lived, how they had shopped, cooked, worshiped, made wagon wheels, printed books, defended themselves, and enforced the law in that early American settlement. When we sat down for dinner at the historic Josiah Chowning's Tavern, we were ready for a treat.

"Good evening," our costumed waitress greeted us. "I would tell you about our special, except we're all out of it. The regular entrees on the menu are good, though. I'll be back for your orders in a minute."

My companions and I looked at each other and laughed. My wife said what we were all thinking: "Gee, if she hadn't told us about the special, we wouldn't be wondering about what we were missing."

It was an illustration of the power of negative thinking. Our waitress had started on the wrong end of the equation. She had emphasized the negative rather than the positive.

We sometimes make the same mistake in business writing. We forget that the affirmative makes a better impression than the negative.

Take, for example, this sentence: "We cannot grant your request for a refund." Now, compare the positive version: "We are unable to grant your request for a refund." Can you hear the difference? (It helps to read the sentences out loud.)

Another way to emphasize the positive is to *de*-emphasize the negative. In writing, this is called s*ubordination*. To illustrate this technique, let's add a second statement to the previous example: "We are unable to grant your request for a refund, but we are sending you a complimentary coupon for a 20% discount on your next purchase."

The second statement is meant to soften the blow and to create goodwill. That's the right idea, but how much better an impression would be made if the first statement were de-emphasized through subordination so that the main emphasis fell on the second statement, like this: "Although we are unable to grant your request for a refund, we are sending you a complimentary coupon for a 20% discount on your next purchase." Subordinating the first statement with the word "although" directs the reader's attention to the second, more positive statement, which is where we want the emphasis to be.

As a rule, positive statements have more impact than negative statements. Consider, for example, these sentences: "It is not common that a poor communicator is promoted" versus "It is rare that a poor communicator is promoted"; "Your service is not reliable" versus "Your service is unreliable"; and "She doesn't often come to work late" versus "She usually comes to work on time."

Likewise, leaders are perceived as being more assertive when they use positive statements. Compare, for example, these sentences: "I don't think we should avoid this issue" versus "I think we should address this issue"; "We don't have any choice but to take action now" versus "We have no choice but to take action now" or, better yet, "We must take action now."

Sometimes the negative element is signified in words other than *not*. Compare, for example, these two statements: "You need to learn new skills to avoid complacency" versus "You need to learn new skills to maintain interest in your job." Or consider the negative tone created by the word *however* in this example: "Our warranty is valid for one year. However, we are willing to extend the warranty for a fee." Now, replace the negative-sounding *however* with the more positive-sounding *in addition* and note the difference: "Our warranty is valid for one year. In addition, we are willing to extend the warranty for a fee."

The moral of the story: If you want to keep people happy, say it in the affirmative. In writing as in life, people would rather be told *what is* than *what is not*.

P.S. The Chesapeake Dinner (sautéed crab cakes served on top of a Virginia ham) that we *did* order was terrific!

Goodwill letters create good feelings in any season

I have a file labeled "kudos." The word comes from the Greek *kydos,* which means fame and renown resulting from an act or an achievement. Its meaning is associated with the notions of glory and praise.

Sometimes, when I'm having a bad day, I pull out my kudos file and thumb through it to cheer myself up. Almost always, it works its magic on me.

My kudos file is not a compilation of achievements in the conventional sense. It consists of notes and letters, words of encouragement and appreciation from friends and associates. It's a collection of things that – well, that just make me feel good.

Take, for example, the oldest document in my file. It's a letter dated April 5, 1979, from James Lindberg, then chair of the Department of Geography at the University of Iowa. It's only four sentences long. It probably took no more than a minute to write, but 13 years later it still makes me feel good when I read it: "Thanks for your recent note. I thoroughly enjoyed participating in the interview process with you. I think you have gotten the Center off to a strong start and we will look forward to working with you on a continuing basis."

That's all it is. But given its context, its author, and its timing, it was a wonderful letter.

I had just been hired to set up the University of Iowa's first campus-wide academic advising program, and some of the departments and faculty were less than enthusiastic about a centralized advising system. I was a young (29), inexperienced administrator just out of graduate school. Professor Lindberg's letter came as a note of reassurance and encouragement.

As I page forward through my feel-good file, each letter brings back warm feelings – not so much for the kind words as for the names of the people who wrote them. Looking back now, I am reminded of something I hope never to forget: It's the relationships that count.

Here is a pink "While you were out" phone slip with a message from a journalism professor who called to compliment me on a series of articles I had written for the *Daily Iowan* on changes in the University's liberal arts curriculum. I was disappointed to have missed his call but saved this record of his one-word message: "Bravo!"

Next come letters of welcome from some of my new colleagues at the University of Minnesota. These are merely courtesy notes, to be sure, but as I thumb through them now I note that the authors' names are the people with whom I ended up having my closest working relationships.

Here is a handwritten note from a staff member who had received a thank-you letter from a student advisee: "I was overwhelmed to find that you had forwarded copies of the 'thank-you' letter from Wendy Wiberg to a number of College administrators. That was most kind of you. I've already received a personal note from [Associate Dean] Roger Page." She was thanking me for circulating a thank-you letter that inspired more thank-you letters in a veritable chorus of thank-yous for a job well done.

One of my favorite goodwill messages is from George Shapiro, Professor of Speech Communication at the University of Minnesota. We had just finished making a presentation to a group of international students. As the students came forward to ask questions and talk with us informally, Professor Shapiro slipped me a note scrawled on the back of his business card: "Steve. Superb job. Thank you. George." In six words he had transformed himself from acquaintance to friend and ally.

So during this holiday season, I offer you this message: Whether you write to recognize the contributions of a staff member, to apologize for a delay in filling an order, or to thank a valued customer for 20 years of business, I offer you kudos for your decency in recognizing the inestimable value of human relationships.

Works Cited / Recommended Reading

Brusaw, Charles T., Gerald J. Alred, and Walter E. Oliu.
***The Business Writer's Handbook.* New York: St. Martin's Press.**
This helpful, easy-to-use handbook features a "unique four-way access system." The main body is organized alphabetically for quick, straightforward reference. If you don't find your topic this way (and sometimes you won't, as when, for example, you're looking for the "nonrestrictive comma"), you can turn to the index, which provides an "exhaustive" (as opposed to "exhausting"?) list of topics. Or if you prefer, you can turn to the topical key, which arranges the alphabetical entries into subject categories, such as "Types of Business Writing" and "Format and Illustrations." Also featured is a section on "Five Steps to Successful Writing" (Preparation, Research, Organization, Writing the Draft, and Revision). Many of the entries are brief, but some (such as formal reports and proofreading) are developed at some length.

Dornan, Edward A., and Charles W. Dawe. *The Brief English Handbook.* **New York: Addison-Wesley.**
More comprehensive in scope than Corbett, this handbook is still compact and easy-to-use, with rules and advice indexed by page tabs in the corners, grammatical terms listed alphabetically in a glossary, cross-referencing, and a complete subject index. It begins with a review of the essentials of grammar before presenting sentence structure, punctuation, and techniques of composition and research. The approach is "necessarily prescriptive in matters of standard English but more relaxed in matters of style." Includes exercises designed to reinforce rules and examples.

Dworsky, Alan L. *The Little Book on Legal Writing.* **Littleton, Colorado: Fred B. Rothman & Co.**
A short handbook that offers advice both on basic writing skills (plain English, style, usage, spelling) and specific applications (case briefs, cases and courts, names, citations, quotations

authority, office memoranda, questions presented, and argument). Each point is illustrated with useful examples, but no exercises are provided.

Elbow, Peter. *Writing Without Teachers.* **New York: Oxford University Press, 1973.**
An excellent book on the process of writing. Discarding the notion that writers first think of what they want to say, then construct an outline, and then write, Elbow believes that thought develops as it is given expression, that we think through the act of writing.

Ewing, David W. *Writing for Results: In Business, Government, and the Professions.* **New York: Wiley.**
Written when Ewing was Executive Editor of the *Harvard Business Review*, this book suggests ways to improve your writing in the context of particular situations. Especially useful are the sections on deciding whether to write (Ewing suggests a seven-item checklist) and on expression (in which he discusses tone, coherence, clarity, correctness, and style).

Gibb, Jack R. "Defensive Communication." *The Journal of Communication.* **Volume 11, number 3, September, 1961, 141-48.**
It was Jack Gibb who in 1961 introduced the notion of defensive versus supportive communication patterns and climates. Since then many people have elaborated and built upon his work. Based on research on small groups, he developed six pairs of defensive and supportive categories (evaluation/description; control/problem orientation; strategy/spontaneity; neutrality/empathy; superiority/equality; and certainty/provisionalism). His theory is that behavior associated with the first characteristics in the pair arouses defensiveness, whereas behavior associated with the second characteristics in the pair reduces defensive feelings.

Goldberg, Natalie, *Writing Down the Bones: Freeing the Writer Within.* **London: Shambhala.**
A wonderfully inspiring book whose main theme is: You *can* write. Goldberg understands the psychological implications of

writing as well as anyone. She urges writers "to learn to trust your own mind and body; to grow patient and nonaggressive." Her practical, imaginative techniques for getting started are a sure antidote to writer's block.

Luey, Beth. *Handbook for Academic Authors.* **New York: Cambridge University Press, 1987.**
This handbook offers thoughtful and practical advice on topics ranging from revising a dissertation and finding a publisher for the scholarly book, to working with a textbook publisher and the mechanics of authorship. Includes an annotated bibliography.

Miller, Casey, and Kate Swift. *The Handbook of Nonsexist Writing for Writers, Editors and Speakers.* **New York: Harper and Row.**
This is more than a handbook to help you avoid sexist language. It is an eloquent, reasoned, erudite argument for ridding our language of its sexually exclusive linguistic structures. With the premise that "every language reflects the prejudices of the society in which it evolved," Miller and Swift take aim at sexually exclusive phrases and wording that suggest that "maleness is the norm, femaleness the deviation."

Rogers, Carl R. **"Barriers and Gateways to Communication."** *The Harvard Business Review,* **July-August, 1952.**
In this important piece, the renowned psychotherapist tries his hand at exploring the relationship between identifying obstacles to communication and providing therapeutic help to individuals with emotional maladjustments. His conclusion: "the major barrier to mutual interpersonal communication is our very natural tendency to judge, to evaluate, to approve (or disapprove) the statement of the other person or the other group."

Shapo, Helene S., Marilyn R. Walter, Elizabeth Fajans. *Writing and Analysis in the Law.* **Westbury, New York: The Foundation Press, Inc.**
A standard textbook that deals with basic writing techniques

(paragraph transitions and development, sentence structure and wording), approaches to legal analysis, and specific applications (the legal memorandum, writing to the court, the appellate brief).

Strunk, William, Jr., and E. B. White. *The Elements of Style.* **New York: Macmillan Co.**
A brief guide offering pithy and practical advice on how to write clear and graceful expository prose. It's a classic — so good that it warrants rereading every couple years.

Sweetnam, Sherry. *The Executive Memo: A Guide to Persuasive Business Communications.* **New York: John Wiley & Sons.**
Designed for the busy practitioner, this book is one of the best on the market. It covers basic principles of communication and persuasion as they apply to everyday writing problems, offers techniques to help you organize your ideas quickly and write faster, and presents models of business communication (information memos, sales letters, proposals, letters of apology, "tough-message" memos) in a straightforward style and format. Its forty-two exercises reinforce and illustrate key points, and its various checklists and index make it easy to use.

Williams, Joseph M. *Style: Ten Lessons in Clarity & Grace.* **Addison Wesley Longman, Inc.**
Eschewing a strictly rule-oriented approach, Williams uses instead the "time-honored" method of copy and imitation to help writers achieve a "mature" style of clarity and grace. The idea is that "simply by writing out the new sentences that result from editing those in the exercises, students will come to feel what it is like to write down a sentence longer than ten or fifteen words." The ten lessons, designed to be taken in "small chunks," one section at a time, deal with clarity, cohesion, emphasis, concision, sprawl, long sentences, elegance, punctuation, and usage.

Wydick, Richard. *Plain English for Lawyers.* **Durham: Carolina Academic Press.**
An excellent brief guide to more understandable legal writing. Each guideline is accompanied by practical exercises.

Zinsser, William. *On Writing Well: An Informal Guide to Writing Nonfiction.* **New York: Harper & Row.**
An excellent discussion of the basic elements of good writing, written by a professor who draws on his experience in teaching a course in nonfiction writing at Yale. Short chapters are devoted to topics such as unity, the lead, and humor. The chapter on simplicity begins with the memorable quote: "Clutter is the disease of American writing."